THE POLITICS OF
CONGRESSIONAL ELECTIONS

THE POLITICS OF
CONGRESSIONAL ELECTIONS

GARY C. JACOBSON
University of California, San Diego

LITTLE, BROWN AND COMPANY
Boston   Toronto

Library of Congress Cataloging in Publication Data

Jacobson, Gary C.
  The politics of congressional elections.

  Bibliography: p. 199
  Includes index.
  1. United States.   Congress—Elections.
I. Title.
JK1067.J3 1983   324′.0973   82-10013
ISBN 0-316-45563-6   AACR2

Library of Congress Catalog Card No. 82-10013

ISBN 0-316-45563-6

9 8 7 6 5 4 3 2

ALP

Published simultaneously in Canada
by Little, Brown & Company (Canada) Limited

Printed in the United States of America

For Marty

Preface

This book is about congressional election politics, broadly understood. In writing it, I have tried to keep in mind that elections are means, not ends in themselves. What happens during campaigns or on election day is, of course, fascinating and important, and I do not neglect congressional candidates, campaigns, and voters. But campaigns and elections are more than curious rituals only because they reflect deeper structural patterns and currents in American political life and help determine how — and how well — we are governed. A considerable part of the book is therefore devoted to tracing the connections between the electoral politics of Congress and other important political phenomena. Examining congressional election politics in this way inevitably raises fundamental questions about representation and responsibility, and these are the central normative concerns of the book. My intent here, then, is to offer a systematic account of what goes on in congressional elections and to show how electoral politics reflect and shape other basic components of the political system, with profound consequences for representative government.

The kind of synthesis I pursue in this book has only become conceivable within the last few years. Two developments have made it possible. First, important new banks of information on congressional voters, candidates, and campaign finances have been assembled; the central questions can now be attacked from a much more solid empirical base. I rely heavily on these new data to make many of the points that form my arguments. Second, congressional scholars have, in recent years, published an extraordinary number of distinguished works touching on various aspects of congressional election politics. I need not mention them here by name; it will quickly become apparent how dependent I am on their insights. These developments, along with the recent shift in national politics exemplified by the Republican takeover of the Senate and the changes in the direction of public policy that have ensued, have conspired to make this a remarkably stimulating time to be thinking and writing about the politics of congressional elections.

I am deeply indebted to the many friends and colleagues who have guided — and corrected — my understanding of congressional election politics. For the past five years I have had the singular good fortune to work as a member of the Committee on Congressional Election Research of the Board of Overseers of National Election Studies; the committee designed the congressional component of the 1978 and 1980 American National Election Studies. That experience was the genesis of this book, and everyone I worked with on the committee has contributed to it in some way: Alan Abramowitz, David Brady, Heinz Eulau, Richard Fenno, John Ferejohn, Morris Fiorina, Barbara Hinckley, Malcolm Jewell, Jack Katosh, James Kuklinski, Thomas Mann, David Mayhew, Warren Miller, Glenn Parker, Barbara Sinclair, Michael Traugott, Raymond Wolfinger, and Gerald Wright.

I am grateful, too, to all of my colleagues at U.C. San Diego for providing an environment wonderfully conducive to scholarly work. Samuel Kernell read and commented on several chapters. I also enjoyed instructive and stimulating conversations with Nathaniel Beck, Peter Cowhey, David Laitin, John Mendeloff, and Samuel Popkin about matters covered in the book.

Morris Fiorina, Herbert Jacob, Burdett Loomis, Thomas Mann, and Steven Rosenstone read the entire manuscript; it is much the better for their many suggestions, and probably the worse for my not having heeded more of them. Will Ethridge, political science editor at Little, Brown, provided just the right combination of encouragement and prodding to see the project through to its completion.

I am obliged also to Denise Gimlin, Edward Lazarus, Del Powell, and David Wilsford for helping to gather some of the data analyzed in Chapter 6, and to Eric Smith of the University of California's State Data Program for tabulating some of the data reported in Table 5.1.

Part of the research reported here was supported by a grant from the National Science Foundation (SES–80–7577), for which I am most grateful. The data used in this book were made available (in part) by the Inter-University Consortium for Political and Social Research. The data for the 1978 and 1980 American National Election Studies were originally collected by the Center for Political Studies of the Institute for Social Research, the University of Michigan, under a grant from the National Science Foundation. Neither the original collectors of the data nor the Consortium bear any responsibility for the analyses or interpretations presented here, and the same, of course, holds for anyone else I have mentioned.

Contents

Tables and Figures

Tables

Figures

THE POLITICS OF
CONGRESSIONAL ELECTIONS

1

Introduction

Elections touch the core of American political life. They provide ritual expression of the myth that makes political authority legitimate: we are governed, albeit indirectly, by our own consent. Elections are also the focus of thoroughly practical politics. They determine who will hold positions of real power in the political system and, by establishing a framework in which power is pursued, profoundly affect the behavior of people holding or seeking power. The mythical and practical components of elections meet at the point where electoral constraints are supposed to make leaders responsive and responsible to the public. How comfortably they fit together has deep consequences for the entire political system. Almost any important development in American political life will be intertwined with the electoral process.

Congressional elections in particular are intimately linked to many basic phenomena of American politics. In countless ways, obvious and subtle, they affect the performance of Congress and, through it, the entire government. At the same time they reflect the changing political landscape, revealing as well as shaping its fundamental contours.

1

The basic questions to be asked about congressional elections are straightforward: Who gets elected to Congress and how? Why do people vote the way they do in congressional elections? How do electoral politics affect the way Congress works and the kinds of policies it produces? What kind of representation do congressional elections really provide? Every answer has further implications for the workings of American politics; and many of them must be traced out in order to grasp the deeper role of congressional elections in the political process.

To explain what goes on in congressional elections and to understand how they are connected in myriad ways to other aspects of American political life are the broad purposes of this book. It also has a more pointed intention: to use a careful examination of the complex, multifaceted business of electing Congress as a unique perspective for understanding some of the roots of present-day political failure and discontent.

The past two decades have been less than happy ones in American political life. Shorthand labels for the most memorable political phenomena compose a dreary litany: assassination; riot; Vietnam; Watergate; OPEC; stagflation; Iran. Every American generation has no doubt found reason to see its times as troubled, uncertain, even retrograde. Nostalgia is historically myopic. But whether or not recent years have delivered more than the usual helping of unwelcome political news, they have certainly shaken Americans' faith in their political leaders and institutions.

Evidence for this distrust abounds. Back in 1964, 76 percent of the American people thought the federal government could be trusted to do what was right most or all of the time; fourteen years later only 24 percent thought so. In 1964 only 29 percent thought that the government was run by a few big selfish interests; by 1980, 77 percent were of that opinion. Forty-seven percent believed in 1964 that government wasted a lot of tax money; 80 percent believed it in 1980. The proportion feeling that people in government are smart and know what they are doing dropped from 69 percent to 35 percent over the same period.[1]

[1] Warren E. Miller, Arthur H. Miller, and Edward J. Schneider, *American National Election Studies Data Sourcebook 1952–1978* (Cambridge: Harvard University Press, 1980), pp. 257–258; 1980 figures are from NES/CPS American National Election Study, 1980.

Examples making the same point could easily be multiplied. No governmental institution has escaped the erosion of public trust. An extraordinary number of people no longer believe their political system and its leaders are capable of coping with basic political problems. And they may be right.

The root causes of political failure and popular disaffection with politics can surely be sought in many fields. But certainly one aspect of political life that demands the closest scrutiny is the process by which leaders are selected. A central argument of this book is, in fact, that political incapacity and public discontent are both connected to a peculiar shortcoming of contemporary congressional election processes: they yield highly responsive yet highly irresponsible political leadership.

It is by no means a simple story. Consider these puzzling conjunctions:

• Although public faith in political institutions and leaders has declined sharply in the last two decades, incumbent members of the House of Representatives win reelection more easily than ever before. We love our congressmen, but we do not love our Congress.[2] Put another way, politicians succeed even though policies fail.

• Even though it is easier to get reelected, more members of Congress are choosing not to try; voluntary retirements were much more common in the 1970s than in the 1960s.

• Although House incumbents are safer than ever, Senate incumbents are not; they have been especially vulnerable in the last few elections.

• Members of Congress are brighter, better educated, harder working, better staffed, with more resources than ever before; yet the image of Congress as ineffectual has never been more widespread.

• Democrats controlled both houses of Congress from 1954 through 1980; a Republican lived in the White House for more than half those years. Each party now controls one house of Congress. Divided control of the federal government was very

---

[2] To paraphrase Richard F. Fenno, Jr. See his "If, As Ralph Nader Says, Congress is 'the Broken Branch,' How Come We Love Our Congressmen So Much?" in *Congress in Change: Evolution and Reform,* ed. Norman J. Ornstein (New York: Praeger, 1975), pp. 277–281.

rare in the fifty years before World War II; it is now the norm.

• Fewer people are bothering to vote even though the impact of government on people is greater and more people share the social characteristics associated with voting than ever before.

Many of these developments are examined more thoroughly in the pages that follow. Ultimately I argue that they are complementary rather than contradictory. They serve at this point to raise questions and suggest themes to be pursued. They also begin to alert us to the range and complexity of interlocking issues that must be dealt with in any thorough account of congressional elections.

The sources of this complexity are many. An important one is the number of different perspectives from which congressional elections can be examined. Consider the alternative ways the question, "How's the congressional election going?" might be answered. A candidate or campaign manager would immediately begin talking about what was going on in the district, who was ahead, what groups were supporting which candidate, how much money was coming in, what issues were emerging. A national party leader — the president, for example — would respond in terms of how many seats the party might gain or lose in the House and Senate and what this might mean for the administration's programs. A private citizen might grumble about the hot air, mudslinging, and general untrustworthiness of politicians, or might scarcely be aware that an election was taking place.

Similarly, political scientists and other people who study congressional elections do so from a variety of research orientations. Some investigate *voters:* Why do people vote the way they do? Why do they vote at all? Others study *candidates and campaigns:* Who runs for Congress, and why? What goes on in campaigns? How is money raised and spent — and what difference does it make? Or they explore the *aggregate results* of congressional elections: What accounts for the national shifts in the vote for congressional candidates of one party or the other? Still others are interested in *representation:* How are the activities of members of Congress, and the performance of Congress as an institution, connected with what goes on in elections? These and other questions are well deserving of individual attention. But it is no less essential to understand how they are all interrelated.

People involved in congressional elections are at least implicitly aware of the connections between the different levels of analysis. Voters are interested primarily in the candidates and campaigns in their state or district, but at least some are conscious of the broader political context and may, for example, adjust their congressional voting decision to their feelings about presidential candidates. Presidents worried about the overall makeup of the Congress are by no means indifferent to individual races and sometimes involve themselves in local campaigns. Candidates and other congressional activists are mindful of national as well as local political conditions they believe influence election outcomes; and of course they spend a great deal of time trying to figure out how to appeal effectively to individual voters.

Scholars, too, are fully aware that, although research strategies dictate that the congressional election terrain be subdivided into workable plots, no aspect of congressional elections can be understood in isolation. It is essential to integrate various streams of investigation for any clear account of what is going on. This is no simple task; a major aim of this book is to determine how far it can be done. One difficulty here is quite familiar to students of the social sciences: how to connect the accounts of individual behavior to large-scale social phenomena. The problem is one of coordinating the micro and macro level accounts of political behavior (there are middle levels, too, of course). But it turns out to be a most fruitful problem; its solution is a rich source of insight into congressional election processes and their consequences.

The approach taken in this book is to examine congressional elections from several perspectives while attending throughout to the interconnections between them. Chapter 2 sets out the legal and institutional context in which congressional elections take place. This formal context is easily taken for granted and overlooked, but it is, on reflection, fundamental. The very existence of congressional elections depends on this structure, and it shapes them in a great many important ways. The chapter also surveys briefly the rich variety of social, economic, and ethnic mixes that are found among states and congressional districts, for this diversity underlies many distinctive aspects of congressional election politics.

The third and fourth chapters examine, respectively, congressional candidates and campaigns. The pervasive effects of incumbency create a theme common to both of these chapters. The resources, strategies, and tactics of candidates vary sharply depending on whether a candidate is an incumbent, a challenger to an incumbent, or running for an open seat, where neither candidate is an incumbent. They also differ between House and Senate candidates in each of these categories. The strategies of candidates in different electoral situations and the consequences of varying strategies are explored. So are the roles of campaign money, organization, campaign activities and tactics, and the local political context. Campaigns both reflect and work to reinforce candidates' assumptions about the electorate, and they are also closely linked to the behavior in office of those elected.

Chapter 5 deals with voting in congressional elections. Knowing who votes and what influences the voting decision are valuable pieces of information in their own right, but such knowledge is even more important as a means for understanding what congressional elections mean, what they can and cannot accomplish. The way voters react is tied closely to the behavior of candidates and the design and operation of campaigns — and to what members of Congress do in office.

The sixth chapter looks upon congressional elections as aggregate phenomena. When all the individual contests are summed up over an election year, the collective outcome determines which party controls the Congress and with how large a majority. It also strongly influences the kinds of national policies that emerge; it is at this level that the government is or is not held responsible. Congressional elections clearly respond to aggregate political conditions. But aggregate outcomes are no more than the summation of individual voting decisions in the districts to election results across all districts. The path that leads from aggregate political conditions to individual voting decisions to aggregate congressional election outcomes is surprisingly complicated; candidates' strategies turn out to provide a critical connecting link.

Finally, of course, congressional elections are important for how they influence the behavior of elected leaders and therefore the success or failure of politics. In fact, the knowledge that they are elected officials is the key to understanding why members of Congress do what they do in office. Not only *that* they are elected, but *how* they are elected matters. How candidates mount campaigns and how voters choose between them has a crucial effect on what members of Congress do with their time and other resources and with the quality, quantity, and direction of their legislative work. Electoral necessities enhance or restrict in predictable ways the influence of individuals, groups, parties, congressional leaders, and presidents. And all of these things affect Congress' performance as a policy-making institution. These arguments are developed in the seventh chapter.

The final chapter assesses Congress as a representative institution. It argues that electoral politics has fostered a system which combines individual responsiveness with collective irresponsibility and suggests that the way in which we elect Congress has contributed mightily to the incapacity of government to deal effectively with pressing national problems and the consequent loss of public faith in political leaders and institutions. It concludes by considering whether the 1980 elections portend any change in the pattern of electoral politics that has developed over the past twenty years and speculates about the interesting possibilities for 1982.

2

The Context

The most striking feature of contemporary congressional elections is the ascendant importance of individual candidates and campaigns. This manifests itself in many ways. Congressional campaigns are overwhelmingly candidate centered. Most serious candidates operate, of choice and necessity, as individual political entrepreneurs. The risks, rewards, and pains of mounting a campaign are largely theirs. They instigate their own candidacies, raise their own resources, and put together their own campaign organizations. Their skills, resources, and strategies have a decisive effect on election outcomes. Voters, for their part, are most strongly influenced by their assessments of the particular candidates running in the state or district. The central focus on individual candidacies has important implications for every aspect of the political process to which congressional elections are relevant. Many are spelled out in subsequent chapters.

This chapter traces some of the roots of candidate-centered electoral politics. It examines the constitutional, legal, and political contexts in which congressional elections take place, for they are fundamental sources of the present system, and it cannot be understood apart from them.

The Constitutional Framework

Whether or not to have an elected legislature was never a question during the constitutional convention that met in Philadelphia in 1787. The influence of British parliamentary tradition and colonial experience — all thirteen colonies had legislatures with at least one popularly elected house — was decisive. Beyond question, the new government would have one. But not much else about it was certain. Delegates disagreed about how the legislative branch would be organized, what its powers would be, and how its members would be selected.

The matter of selection involved several important issues. The most crucial was the basis of representation: how were seats in the legislature to be apportioned? Delegates from large states naturally preferred representation according to population; otherwise, their constituents would be underrepresented. Those from smaller states were convinced that their interests would be in jeopardy if only numbers counted, so they proposed equal representation for each state. The controversy coincided with another unsettled and unsettling issue: was it to be a national government representing a national citizenry, or was it to be a federal government representing sovereign states? [1]

The conflict was resolved by a quintessential political deal. General sentiment was strongly in favor of a bicameral legislature,[2] and this made a solution easier. Each side got what it wanted. Seats in one chamber, the House of Representatives, would be apportioned by population; each state's representation would be determined by its share of the population as measured in a decennial census (Article I, Section 2). In the other chamber, the Senate, states would enjoy equal representation, each choosing two senators (Article I, Section 3).

This "great compromise," as it has been called, opened the way to resolving another dispute. At issue was the extent of popular participation in electing officials in the new government. Most delegates were skeptical of democracy as they conceived

[1] See James Madison, Alexander Hamilton, and John Jay, *The Federalist,* ed. Edward Meade Earle (New York: Modern Library, 1937) Nos. 37 and 39.

[2] Ten of the thirteen colonies and, of course, Britain, had bicameral legislatures.

it, but to varying degrees. A bicameral legislature allowed different levels of popular involvement in choosing members of Congress. Representatives were to be "popularly" [3] chosen in frequent elections. Biennial elections were the compromise choice between the annual elections proposed by many delegates and the three-year term advocated by James Madison.[4] Broad suffrage and short terms were intended to ensure that one branch of government, the House, remained as close as possible to the people.

The Senate, in contrast, was designed to be much more insulated from momentary shifts in the public mood. The term of office was set at six years (another compromise; terms of three, four, five, six, seven, and nine years had been proposed [5]). Continuity was enhanced by having one-third of the Senate's membership elected every two years. Senators, furthermore, were to be chosen by state legislatures rather than by voters. The Senate could thus act as a stable and dispassionate counterweight to the more popular and radical House, protecting the new government from the volatility thought to be characteristic of democracies. Its structure could also embody the elements of state sovereignty that remained.[6]

The opposition to popular democracy expressed in the indirect election of senators (and the president) diminished during the nineteenth century. Restrictions on suffrage were gradually lifted, and more and more offices came to be filled by popular election. The Civil War effectively settled the issue of national sovereignty. By the beginning of this century the constitutional method of choosing senators seemed anachronistically undemocratic to most Americans, and it was replaced, through the Seventeenth Amendment, ratified in 1913, by popular election. Members of both houses of Congress are now chosen in elections

[3] The Constitution specifies that "Electors in each State shall have the Qualifications requisite for the Electors of the most numerous Branch of the State Legislature" (Article I, Section 2). Property and other qualifications were in fact common in the early years of the nation; universal suffrage took a long time to achieve.

[4] *Electing Congress* (Washington, D.C.: Congressional Quarterly, Inc., 1978), p. 135.

[5] Ibid.

[6] Madison, Hamilton, and Jay, *The Federalist,* No. 62.

in which nearly every citizen past his eighteenth birthday is eligible to vote.[7]

Congressional Districts

The Constitution itself apportioned seats among states for the first Congress (Article I, Section 3). Following the initial census in 1790, membership of the House was set at 105, with each state given one seat for each 33,000 inhabitants. Until 1911, the House grew as population increased and new states were added. Congress avoided the painful duty of reducing any state's representation in response to population shifts by adding seats after each decennial census. Eventually a point was reached where further growth could seriously impair the House's efficiency. Membership was set at 435 after the 1910 census, and strong opposition developed to any further increase.

A crisis thus arrived with the 1920 census results. Large population shifts between 1910 and 1920 and a fixed House membership would mean that many states — and members of Congress — would lose seats. Adding to the turmoil was the discovery by the census that, for the first time, a majority of Americans lived in urban rather than rural areas. Reapportionment was certain to increase the political weight of city dwellers and reduce that of farmers. The result was an acrimonious stalemate that was not resolved until 1929, when a law was passed establishing a permanent system for reapportioning the 435 House seats after each census; it would be carried out, if necessary, without additional legislation.[8]

The new system took effect after the 1930 census. Because twenty years had passed since the last apportionment, unusually large shifts occurred. California's delegation went from eleven to twenty; other big gainers were Michigan (four), Texas (three), and New York, Ohio, and New Jersey (two each).

[7] The exceptions are people in penal and other institutions and, in many states, former felons. Senate seats vacated by retirement, death, or resignation before the end of the term may be filled by gubernatorial appointment until the next regular general election; vacated House seats are filled by special elections.

[8] *Congressional Quarterly's Guide to U.S. Elections* (Washington, D.C.: Congressional Quarterly, Inc., 1976), pp. 530–34.

Twenty-one states lost seats; Missouri lost three and four other states lost two.[9] Subsequent shifts have not been so dramatic, but the beginning of each decade still ushers in a period of heightened uncertainty and anxiety among congressional incumbents. Anxiety is not unwarranted. In 1972, for example, eight of the thirteen incumbents who were defeated could trace their loss to redistricting; in three cases, two incumbents were thrown into the same district.

At least a dozen incumbents were thrown into districts with other incumbents in the redistricting that followed the 1980 census. This happened most often, but not exclusively, in states which had lost representation through reapportionment. As in past decades, the new distribution of House seats reflects population shifts since the previous census. Doing so, it redistributes power among states and regions. States of the East and Midwest lost a total of seventeen seats to states of the South and West. Southern and western states now control a bare majority — 218 of 435 seats — in the House.

At first federal law fixed only the number of representatives each state could elect; other important aspects of districting were left to the states. Until 1842, single-member districts were not required by law, and a number of states used multi-member or at-large districts. Thereafter, apportionment legislation usually required that states establish contiguous single-member districts and, in some years, required that they be of roughly equal populations and even "compact" in shape. Such requirements were never, when challenged, successfully enforced. Single-member districts became the overwhelming norm, but districts composed of "contiguous and compact territory . . . containing as nearly as practicable an equal number of inhabitants," in the words of the 1901 reapportionment act, did not.[10]

Many states continued to draw districts with widely differing populations. In 1930, for example, New York's largest district (766,425) contained nearly nine times as many people as its smallest (90,671). As recently as 1962, the most populous district in Michigan (802,994) had 4.5 times the inhabitants of its

9 Ibid.
10 Ibid., p. 528.

least populous (177,431).[11] Rural populations were usually over-represented at the expense of people living in cities and suburbs. The Supreme Court's ruling in *Wesberry* v. *Sanders* (376 U.S. 1), however, applied the principle of one person–one vote to congressional districts, and since then malapportioned districts have, under the watchful eye of the courts, become extinct.

The Court's rulings have indeed given more equal weight to each citizen's House vote, but they have also reinforced some less desirable aspects of the congressional election system. Drawing district lines with an eye to numbers rather than to natural political communities increases the number of districts composed of people with nothing in common save residence in the district. District boundaries are even less likely than before to coincide with the local political divisions — cities, counties, state legislative districts — around which parties are organized. So a greater number of congressional aspirants become political orphans, left to their own organizational devices. More will be said later about the widespread irrelevance of local parties to congressional candidates; the structure of House districts is clearly one of its sources.

The requirement of equal district populations has not interfered with another old political custom: gerrymandering. District boundaries are not politically neutral. Parties controlling state governments are naturally tempted to draw district lines designed to maximize the number of seats the party can win, given the number and distribution of its usual voters. They do this by concentrating the opposing party's voters in a small number of districts which that party can win by large margins, thus "wasting" many of its votes, and by creating as many districts as possible where their own party has a solid, though not overwhelming, majority.

The political consequences of the partisan gerrymander can be dramatic — and devastating for the minority party. The redistricting of Indiana following the 1980 census provides a remarkable example. Republicans, controlling the State House and the legislature, were open in their intentions: "They [Democrats] are going to have to face the political reality that we are

[11] Ibid., p. 530.

going to do everything we can to hurt them," said the chairman of the state senate's Elections Committee, Charles E. Bosma.[12] It was no idle threat. Bosma's committee produced one new district that contained the homes of three Democratic incumbents. Two Democrats had their districts chopped up and redistributed to four new districts. All five of the Democrats planning to seek reelection had to move their place of residence to have any chance at all; the remaining incumbent Democrat gave up and decided to run for statewide office. The Democrat's six–five majority in Indiana's House delegation was expected to become a four–six or three–seven minority after the 1982 elections (Indiana lost a seat through reapportionment).[13]

Partisan advantage is not the only principle guiding redistricting; Bosma was careful to design a district where he would be a strong candidate should he decide to run for Congress.[14] This is not unusual. An observer of New Jersey politics put it this way: "You have 120 guys down there [in the state legislature], all of whom figure they should be congressmen. Sometimes party interests or the interests of incumbent congressmen fall by the wayside." [15]

When both parties share control of state government, neither can turn redistricting to partisan advantage. Usually an arrangement is worked out that protects the incumbents of both parties, subject, again, to modifications that serve the ambitions of state legislators. Congressional incumbents are sometimes allowed to draw the districts themselves.[16]

The politics of redistricting are often complicated by personal squabbles. During the most recent redistricting of Massachusetts, for example, a Democratic governor and state legislature combined the districts of Barney Frank, a Democrat, and Margaret Heckler, a Republican, in a way that favored Heckler.

[12] "Redistricting: Gov. Gerry's Monuments," *Congressional Quarterly Weekly Report* 39 (May 9, 1981):811.
[13] "Classic Gerrymander by Indiana Republicans," *C.Q. Weekly Report* 39 (October 17, 1981):2017–2022.
[14] "Courts Could Be Called On to Settle Partisan Squabbling in Several Midwestern States," *C.Q. Weekly Report* 39 (May 2, 1981):758–759.
[15] "Redistricting Procedure Has Few Rules," *C.Q. Weekly Report* 39 (February 21, 1981):354.
[16] Ibid.

About three-quarters of the people in the new district had been her constituents, only one-quarter his. Frank's protests were ignored, partly because he had been a maverick state legislator and was not warmly remembered by his former colleagues, partly because the governor, Edward J. King, feared that if Heckler's new district were too difficult for her to win, she would run against him for governor instead.[17]

Gerrymandering occasionally produces bizarrely-shaped districts; the term itself comes from a cartoon depicting an odd, salamander-like creature suggested by a district drawn under the administration of Elbridge Gerry, an early governor of Massachusetts. A modern example is the 8th congressional district of Missouri which, "after five redistrictings in fifteen years, has at last got a fairly regular shape. Before the 1972 redistricting, it looked like a slingshot; today it looks rather like a chocolate rooster with a solid base." [18]

These comments on districting would not seem to apply to the Senate. It's "districts" are fixed by state boundaries, and the question of reapportionment never arises. It is easy to find examples of state boundaries that cut across natural economic units — greater New York City, with suburbs in Connecticut and New Jersey, forms such a unit — and states that are sharply divided into distinct and conflicting political regions (Tennessee, for example). But this matters less because states are, after all, important political units for purposes other than Senate elections. Indeed, this is an important basis for some of the differences between House and Senate elections that are spelled out in later chapters.

Election Laws

The diversity that once characterized state election laws has gradually given way to substantially greater uniformity, but important differences can still be identified. Congress was given

---

[17] "Campaign '82: Frank Weakened by New Map," *C.Q. Weekly Report* 39 (December 19, 1981):2541.

[18] Michael Barone, Grant Ujifusa, and Douglas Matthews, *The Almanac of American Politics 1980* (New York: E.P. Dutton, 1979), p. 503.

the constitutional power to regulate all federal elections (Article I, Section 4), but was in no hurry to do so. At first, states were allowed to go entirely their own way. For example, at one time many states elected members of Congress in odd-numbered years; the practice did not entirely end until 1880. The date of federal elections was not fixed as the first Tuesday after the first Monday in November until 1845 (and states could still hold elections on a different date if their constitutions so required). For a time some states required the winner of a congressional election to receive a majority of all votes cast; now all states permit election by plurality, at least in general elections. Restrictions on suffrage once varied from state to state; constitutional amendments, court decisions, and federal laws have now eliminated almost every restriction on suffrage for citizens who have passed their eighteenth birthday.

The trend toward more uniform election laws is not merely of historical interest. A single date for all federal elections, for instance, encourages national campaigns, party tickets, and coattail effects. Each election is more than an isolated, idiosyncratic event, or at least it can be treated as such by voters. The removal of formal and informal barriers to voting has substantially altered the political complexion of some areas, notably in the deep south, where formerly excluded black voters are now an important political force. Lowering the voting age to eighteen has made the student vote a key factor in districts encompassing large university towns like Ann Arbor, Michigan, and Madison, Wisconsin.

The process of voting itself has undergone important changes. Prior to the 1890s, each party produced its own ballots, listing only its own candidates, which were handed to voters outside the polling place. The party ballots were readily distinguishable; voting was thus a public act. Ballot forms also made it difficult for voters to split their tickets — that is, to vote for candidates of more than one party — for this required manipulating several ballots. The system invited intimidation of voters and other forms of corruption; it was replaced in a remarkable burst of reform between 1888 and 1896, when about 90 percent of the states adopted what was called the Australian Ballot (after the country of its origin). An Australian Ballot is produced by the government, lists candidates from all parties, and is marked in the privacy of a voting booth.[19]

One immediate consequence of this change was a notable increase in ticket splitting. But the degree of increase depended on what kind of Australian ballot was adopted. The "office bloc" ballot, which lists candidates by office, encourages more ticket splitting than does the "party column" ballot, which lists candidates by party. Beyond using the party column, the ballot can foster straight ticket voting by allowing voters to mark a single spot (or pull a single lever on a voting machine) to vote for all the party's candidates. Differences among ballot types, and their consequences, persist to this day.[20]

Again, variations in formal procedures are politically consequential. The effects of Australian Ballot reform generally run counter to those of uniform election dates but vary with the type of Australian Ballot used. Easier ticket splitting weakens coattail effects and other partisan links between candidates. It helps to focus the election on candidates rather than parties. And the focus on candidates is, it will become clear, a predominant characteristic of contemporary congressional elections.

Political Parties

Without question the most important additions to the institutional framework established by the Constitution have been political parties. The parties, along with the system of presidential elections which inspired their development, are the formal institutions that contribute most to making congressional elections other than purely local festivals and politicians other than purely independent political entrepreneurs. The evident atrophy of party organizations and weakening of partisan ties over the

[19] Jerrold G. Rusk, "The Effect of the Australian Ballot Reform on Split Ticket Voting: 1876–1908," in *Controversies in American Voting Behavior*, eds. Richard G. Niemi and Herbert F. Weisberg (San Francisco: W.H. Freeman, 1976), pp. 485–486.
[20] Rusk, "Australian Ballot Reform," pp. 493–509; Angus Campbell, Philip E. Converse, Warren E. Miller, and Donald E. Stokes, *The American Voter* (New York: John Wiley, 1960), p. 276.

past several decades is thus a crucial factor in the detachment of congressional elections from national political forces and in the rise of candidate-centered campaigns.

The decline of parties can be attributed to a variety of causes; several of the more important ones are discussed later on. A fundamental factor, however, is clearly institutional: the rise and spread of primary elections as the method for choosing party nominees for the general election. Nineteenth-century parties nominated candidates in caucuses and, later, conventions. These were often dominated by self-elected party elites; they came under increasing criticism when the United States entered into a period of sectional one-party dominance following the election of 1896. Parties faced with serious competition found it in their own interest to nominate attractive candidates; without this constraint — with the assurance of victory because of an overwhelming local majority — they could freely nominate incompetent hacks or worse. With the nomination tantamount to election in so many places, the general election, and therefore the voter, seemed increasingly irrelevant.

The direct primary election was introduced as a way to weaken party bosses by transferring the right to choose the party's nominees to the party's voters and to allow people to cast a meaningful vote in the face of meaningless general elections. In the south, where one-party dominance was most pronounced, most states eventually established a second, runoff primary between the two candidates receiving the most votes if none wins a majority on the first ballot. Today election laws in every state provide for primary elections for House and Senate nominations — though the rules governing them vary from state to state — and party leaders are able to control the nomination in very few places.

A few states still hold nominating conventions and require that candidates receive a minimum vote at the convention (20 percent is the usual threshold) to be eligible for the primary ballot. But even this may not give the party much control. In one convention state, Colorado, the eventual Republican nominee for the Senate in 1980, Mary Buchanan, did not win support of 20 percent of the delegates, but she got on the primary ballot anyway by petition. She defeated three other Republicans, all of whom were preferred by party leaders, then lost the general election.[21]

Scattered instances of party control over congressional nominations can still be found. When the congressman who represented Illinois' 5th District (in Chicago) died in 1975, state representative John Fary "was called into Mayor Daley's office. At 65, Fary had been a faithful servant of the machine; and he thought the Mayor was going to tell him it was time to retire. Instead, he was told he was going to Congress." [22] He did, declaring on the night of his special election victory, "I will go to Washington to help represent Mayor Daley. For twenty-one years I represented the Mayor in the legislature, and he was always right." [23] When, in 1982, Fary ignored the party's request that he retire, he was crushed in the primary.

Fary's tale is noteworthy because it is so far from the normal. The party organization's influence on congressional nominations varies but is generally feeble. Few congressional candidates find opposition from the local party leaders to be a significant handicap; neither is their support very helpful. The nomination is not something to be awarded by the party but rather a prize to be fought over (when it seems worth having) by freebooting political privateers.

Primary elections have largely deprived parties of their most important source of influence over elected officials. They no longer control access to the ballot and, therefore, to political office. They cannot determine who runs under the party's label and so cannot control what the label represents. National parties have never had much influence in the nominating process, and this has long been an important barrier to strong party discipline in Congress. American parties lack a crucial sanction available to their European counterparts: the ability to deny renomination to uncooperative members. Now state and local parties typically have few sanctions and little influence.

[21] "The Outlook: Senate, House and Governors," *C.Q. Weekly Report* 38 (October 11, 1980):2999.

[22] Barone et al., *Almanac*, p. 246.

[23] Alan Ehrenhalt, ed., *Politics in America: Members of Congress in Washington and at Home* (Washington, D.C.: Congressional Quarterly Press, 1981), p. 333.

The primary election system also complicates the pursuit of a congressional career. Candidates must be prepared to face two distinct, if overlapping, electorates. They are thereby compelled to pay more heed to local than to national concerns.

Differences in primary election laws underlie much of the diversity among congressional election processes across states. The date of the general election may be fixed, but primaries are held at any time from March through October. The runoff primary used in ten southern states has already been mentioned; where two-party competition has finally developed, candidates must sometimes win three serious contests to gain office. In 1974, for example, Robert Krueger took the 21st District of Texas after three close contests. He finished second in the first primary with 32 percent of the vote; won the runoff primary with 52 percent; and won the general election with 54 percent. He spent almost $360,000 (more than $600,000 in today's dollars) doing it, the most spent by any winning House candidate that year.[24] Rules governing access to the ballot differ; some states require only a small fee and virtually anyone can run; others require a larger fee or some minimum number of signatures on a petition. Frivolous candidacies are thus encouraged or discouraged to differing degrees.

This discussion of the legal and institutional framework of congressional elections has necessarily been brief; filling in all the details would demand volumes. But it is sufficient to alert us to some of the important ways in which reference to the formal context is required to account for the activities of candidates, voters, and other participants in congressional elections.

It is important to remember that the formal context does not arrive mysteriously from somewhere outside the political system. Rules and institutions are consciously created and shaped by politically active people. Rules that encourage members of Congress to pursue their aims independently of their party evolve because voters and politicians value independence. So although

[24] Robert L. Lineberry, John E. Sinclair, Lawrence C. Dodd, and Alan M. Sager, "The Case of the Wrangling Professors," in *The Making of Congressmen: Seven Campaigns of 1974,* ed. Alan Clem (North Scituate, Massachusetts: Duxbury Press, 1976), pp. 167–208.

in the short view it seems that the formal framework establishes a set of independent parameters to which political actors are forced to adapt, it does not. Rather, the framework itself reflects the values and preferences prevalent among politically active citizens, and it changes as these change.

Social and Political Contexts

Rules and customs controlling districting and primary elections may contribute to the large idiosyncratic component of congressional elections, but the contribution is hardly decisive. Idiosyncracy is deeply rooted in the cultural, economic, and geographical heterogeneity of the United States. A few short examples will suggest the astonishing variety of electoral conditions that would-be candidates must be prepared to deal with. States and districts vary in:[25]

Size. Simple geography is an abundant source of variation. House districts are as small as a few city blocks (New York's 18th District) or as large as Alaska's 586,000 square miles, where campaigning by airplane is essential, and occasionally fatal.[26] Even Michigan has a district that is more than 477 miles from end to end (the 11th). The range among states is smaller but still enormous. The purely physical problems of campaigning in or representing constituencies differ greatly and can be quite severe.

Population. Obviously, states vary widely in population, and both districts and states also vary in population density. Imagine the problems faced by California's senators, who are expected to represent 23,000,000 people living more than 2,500 miles from Washington, D.C. It is probably no coincidence that in the last fifty years only two of California's senators have won more than two terms. Alaska's senators serve only 400,000 people, but they

[25] All of the examples discussed below are taken from Barone et al., *Almanac.* They refer to districts of the 1970's.

[26] House Majority Leader Hale Boggs and Alaska's congressman, Nick Begich, were killed in a plane crash while campaigning in that state in 1972.

are even further from the capitol and are scattered over a far larger area. Rhode Island, in contrast, is "the closest thing we have to a city state," [27] compact, with a relatively small population.

Economic Base. Sixty percent of the workers in the 7th District of Michigan get their paycheck from General Moters; 38 percent of those in Maryland's 5th District work for the federal government; 35 percent of those in South Carolina's 1st District are on the military payroll. Delaware is the home of DuPont, with annual revenues of $10 billion compared to the state government's $500 million income. At the other extreme are states and districts with thoroughly heterogeneous local economies.

Income. According to the 1970 census, the poorest district in the nation is Kentucky's 5th; its median income at that time was $4,669. The wealthiest, by many measures, is Maryland's 8th, with a median income of $17,102. The Kentucky district voted for Gerald Ford in 1976 and is represented in the House by a Republican; the Maryland district has gone Democratic in four of the last five presidential elections and is served in the House by a Democrat.

Communications. Peoria is at the center of Illinois' 18th District; its newspapers and television and radio stations cover the district so efficiently that it is a favorite test market for new products: will it play in Peoria? Compare it to any of the thirty-five or so districts that fall into the New York City media market or to a state like Wyoming, with multiple media markets. Or consider New Jersey, a state of more than 7 million people with no VHF television station and no major newspaper of its own. Campaigning — and representing — *are* largely communication. It is easy to see how the structure of media markets determines which tactical options are available to candidates. But more subtle influences operate as well; in some districts, for example, a member of Congress is a newsworthy politician; in others, he or she is lost in the crowd.

[27] Barone et al., *Almanac,* p. 785.

Ethnicity. Some districts are overwhelmingly of one racial or ethnic group. Nearly all the residents of the 1st District of Illinois are black; most in California's 25th District are Hispanic. Some districts are composed of an ethnic patchwork, like California's 5th, which in 1970 was 12 percent black, 18 percent Hispanic, 8 percent Chinese, 5 percent Italian, 4 percent Filipino, and included a few Samoans for good measure; about 25 percent were white, English-speaking, third-generation Americans. States, too, have very different ethnic mixes; the political importance of Jews in New York or Irish in Massachusetts or Hispanics in New Mexico are familiar examples.

Age. The median age in Florida's 6th District (St. Petersburg) was fifty-eight in 1970; 39 percent of the voters were over sixty-five. Compare this to a district like Michigan's 2nd (Ann Arbor, Ypsilanti), where 15 percent of the voters are college students and the median voting age is nearly twenty years younger. Imagine how the dominant political concerns differ between the two.

Political Customs. Some states and districts have historic traditions of strong loyalty to candidates of one party or the other; others are characterized by intense two-party competition. Still others seem perversely independent; the 5th District of Florida managed to elect a nonincumbent Democrat during the 1972 Nixon landslide and a Republican in the Watergate year of 1974. Turnout in recent elections has been as low as 11 percent (in the 21st District of New York in 1978; its current representative won a special election in 1978 with a total of 7,959 votes of the 13,753 cast and has not been opposed since) and as high as 77 percent. The range for Senate elections is narrower — 19 to 54 percent in 1978, 45 to 70 percent in 1976 — but it is still striking.

These categories and examples do not begin to exhaust the possibilities but they are sufficient to make the point: politically relevant conditions vary enormously across states and districts and are a potent source of particularism and idiosyncracy in the electoral politics of Congress. The problem for each congressional aspirant is to devise a strategy to win and maintain the support of voters in a *particular* state or district, and it is not surprising that no common formula has been discovered. Nor is it surprising that necessity has turned independence into a primary virtue claimed by candidates. But recognition of the heterogeneity among states and districts cannot explain why fragmentation and independence *increased* during the 1960s and 1970s; the pull has always been there; why did it become less resistable?

3

Congressional Candidates

Each state or congressional district is a unique electoral arena. Diversity among constituencies underlies the astonishing variety of political forces operating in congressional politics. But when attention is shifted to particular states or districts, as it is when we examine congressional candidates and campaigns — the subjects of this and the next chapter — the local context becomes a constant rather than a variable factor. Its elements are fixed, at least for the short run. Electoral variation arises elsewhere: in the skills, resources, and strategies of candidates and other participants in the politics of congressional elections. And all of these are linked in important ways to a single phenomenon: incumbency. Incumbency is by no means a simple, unidimensional factor, however. This is immediately apparent from its very different impact in House and Senate elections, but its complexities extend well beyond this difference.

The Incumbency Factor

Incumbency stands out as a conspicuous factor in House elections from almost any perspective. Most obviously, incumbency is a dominant consideration because incumbents are so

25

consistently successful at winning elections, and anyone involved in politics knows it. At a deeper level, nearly everything pertaining to candidates and campaigns for the House of Representatives is profoundly influenced by whether the candidate is an incumbent, challenging an incumbent, or pursuing an open seat. And understanding why incumbents do so well is central to comprehending the strengths and weaknesses of the House as an institution.

The basic picture could not be clearer. The data in Table 3.1 show just how thoroughly incumbency dominates the outcomes of House elections. Typically, more than 90 percent of the candidates are incumbents, and more than 90 percent of them win. On the average, fewer than 2 percent of incumbents are defeated in primary elections; fewer than 7 percent lose in general elections. Even in years very unfavorable to a party, a large majority of its House incumbents return. In 1974 for example, 78 percent of the Republican incumbents in the House survived general election challenges; the equivalent figure for House Democrats in 1980 was 89 percent.[1]

As striking as these figures are, the impact of incumbency in House elections is not exhausted by bare reelection rates. From other evidence it is clear that House incumbents have enjoyed a notable increase in security since the mid 1960s. They win only slightly more frequently now — not much room for improvement remained — but they do win by wider margins. Prior to 1966, about two-thirds of the House incumbents won with more than 60 percent of the two-party vote. Since then, more than 75 percent have done so. David Mayhew has analyzed the development over time of a strongly bimodal distribution of vote percentages in elections involving House incumbents in graphic detail. The deepening trough in the distribution is centered on the marginal range of 40 to 60 percent. The graphs in Figure 3.1, based on data from two elections that bracket the period of change, 1948 and 1972, depict what has happened. A much smaller percentage of contests involving incumbents were closely fought in 1972 than in 1948. This decline in competition is apparent only in contests for seats held by incumbents; by the

---

[1] Nineteen seventy-four was a notoriously bad year for Republican congressional candidates; 1980 was a particularly bad year for Democrats.

TABLE 3.1
Reelection Rates of House and Senate Incumbents, 1946–1980

Year	Seeking Reelection	Defeated in Primaries	Defeated in General Election	Percentage Reelected
House				
1946	398	18	52	82
1948	400	15	68	79
1950	400	6	32	91
1952	389	9	26	91
1954	407	6	22	93
1956	411	6	16	95
1958	396	3	37	90
1960	405	5	25	93
1962	402	12	22	92
1964	397	8	45	87
1966	411	8	41	88
1968	409	4	9	97
1970	401	10	12	95
1972	390	12	13	94
1974	391	8	40	88
1976	384	3	13	96
1978	382	5	19	94
1980	388	6	31	91
Senate				
1946	30	6	7	57
1948	25	2	8	60
1950	32	5	5	69
1952	31	2	9	65
1954	32	2	6	75
1956	29	0	4	86
1958	28	0	10	64
1960	29	0	1	97
1962	35	1	5	83
1964	33	1	4	85
1966	32	3	1	88
1968	28	4	4	71
1970	31	1	6	77
1972	27	2	5	74
1974	27	2	2	85
1976	25	0	9	64
1978	25	3	7	60
1980	29	4	9	55

Sources: 1946–1978: John F. Bibby, Thomas E. Mann, and Norman Ornstein, *Vital Statistics on Congress, 1980* (Washington, D.C.: American Enterprise Institute for Public Policy Research, 1980), Tables 1–7 and 1–8. Reprinted by permission. *1980: Congressional Quarterly Weekly Report* 38 (November 8, 1980), pp. 3302, 3320–3321.

FIGURE 3.1
House Vote in Districts with Incumbents Running, 1948 and 1972

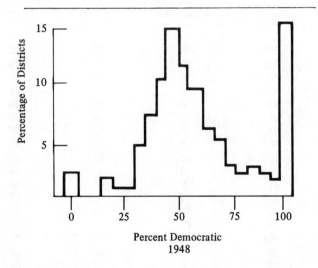

Percent Democratic
1948

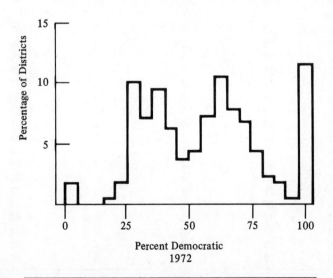

Percent Democratic
1972

Source: Morris P. Fiorina, "The Decline of Collective Responsibility in American Politics." Reprinted by permission of *Daedalus,* Journal of the American Academy of Art and Sciences, Vol. 109, Summer 1980, Boston, MA.

same measures, contests for open seats have remained thoroughly competitive.[2]

Other research has reinforced the same point. One indication of the value of incumbency is what happens when a candidate runs as an incumbent for the first time. The average gain in the percentage of the vote between a member's first and second election, adjusted for national trends, was +2.7 from 1962 through 1966, +6.6 from 1968 through 1974. Another index is what happens when the incumbent retires; the falloff in the vote percentage won by the candidate of the retiring incumbent's party averaged −2.2 in the earlier period, −7.7 later.[3] A separate study concluded that the value of running as an incumbent increased from 2 to 5 percent of the vote about 1966.[4]

The story is rather different for Senate incumbents. As the data in Table 3.1 indicate, senators have not been so consistently successful, although election odds still favor them. There was a sharp drop in the proportion of Senate incumbents defeated in general elections in the 1960s, but this was reversed in the 1970s. The 1980 election provided striking proof of the greater vulnerability of incumbent senators; only 54 percent of the incumbent Democrats won. Senate contests are also much more likely to be close; most Senate seats are won with less than 60 percent of the vote. The average vote advantage enjoyed by incumbent senators did increase during the 1960s,[5] but that pattern has not been maintained in the most recent decade.

The House-Senate differences make it clear that incumbency has no simple, uniform impact on congressional election outcomes. Even in House elections, some incumbents lose. The shift

[2] These years are typical of their periods; the tall columns to the right (Figure 3.1), at 100 percent, represent uncontested seats. See David R. Mayhew, "Congressional Elections: The Case of the Vanishing Marginals," *Polity* 6 (1974):298–301.

[3] Albert D. Cover and David R. Mayhew, "Congressional Dynamics and the Decline of Competitive Congressional Elections," in *Congress Reconsidered*, eds. Lawrence C. Dodd and Bruce I. Oppenheimer (New York: Praeger, 1977), p. 60.

[4] Robert E. Erikson, "Malapportionment, Gerrymandering, and Party Fortunes in Congressional Elections," *American Political Science Review* 66 (1972):1240.

[5] Warren Lee Kostroski, "Party and Incumbency in Postwar Senate Elections: Trends, Patterns, and Models," *American Political Science Review* 67 (1973):1228.

in votes for incumbents from one election to the next is, in fact, highly variable. For example, the average vote shift between 1972 and 1974 for seats contested by incumbents was 8.2 percentage points Democratic; but the range of shifts was more than 36 percentage points for both Republicans and Democrats.[6] The electoral effects of incumbency are by no means uniform either across districts or in the same district across elections.

These observations raise a number of questions central to the study of congressional elections. Why do incumbents usually do so well? Why do House incumbents do so much better than Senate incumbents? Why are more House incumbents winning by wide margins now than they were prior to the mid-1960s? Why does the electoral value of incumbency vary so much among incumbents? The answers are crucial to understanding congressional politics as well as congressional elections. They involve a complicated, interlocking set of institutional, behavioral, and contextual elements which require detailed analysis.

The institutional characteristics of Congress are a good place to begin. They have been examined most closely by David Mayhew, whose basic conclusion is stated succinctly: "if a group of planners sat down and tried to design a pair of American national assemblies with the goal of serving members' reelection needs year in and year out, they would be hard pressed to improve on what exists." [7]

The congressional system permits the widest individual latitude for pursuing reelection strategies. Take organization as one example. The highly decentralized committee and subcommittee structure allows members to specialize in legislative areas where they can best serve local interests. It also provides most members with a solid piece of the legislative turf. The operative norm for writing legislation is similar: something for everyone. Positive-sum politics, represented by the pork barrel and the christmas tree bill (one with separate little "gifts" for a variety of special interest groups), is much more prevalent than the

[6] And the standard deviation from the mean was as large as the mean itself. See Thomas E. Mann, *Unsafe at Any Margin: Interpreting Congressional Elections* (Washington, D.C.: American Enterprise Institute for Public Policy Research, 1977), p. 90.

[7] David R. Mayhew, *Congress: The Electoral Connection* (New Haven: Yale University Press, 1974), pp. 81–82.

zero-sum competition for scarce resources. Members defer to each other's requests for particular benefits for their states or districts in return for deference to their own.

The parties also bow to the varied electoral needs of members. Party discipline within Congress is minimal. In the face of controversial and divisive issues, "the best service a party can supply to its congressmen is a negative one: it can leave them alone. And this is in general what the congressional parties do." [8] Party leaders take the position that the first duty is to get reelected and encourage members to "vote the district first," which they happily do.

The system allows members to take the "right" positions, make pleasing statements, and bring home some bacon without taking any responsibility for the collective performance of Congress. It provides a setting for emphasizing individual achievements while insulating members from blame for the general failures and inadequacies of the institution, which are at least in part a consequence of the patterns of behavior encouraged by the system itself. This is important, because the public's assessment of Congress' performance is consistently and strongly negative. Ratings of Congress actually declined during the same period in which House incumbents have been winning by larger margins, an irony that has not passed unnoticed. People rate their congressmen far higher than their Congress.[9]

Members of Congress have also given themselves an astonishing array of official resources that can be used to pursue reelection. These include salary, travel, office, staff, and communication allowances that are now conservatively estimated to be worth more than $1 million over a two-year House term.[10] All have been augmented dramatically during the past two decades. The growth in personal staffs of members of the House and Senate since 1930 is documented in Table 3.2. The sharpest increase occurred between 1957 and 1976. Travel allowances have grown in a comparable fashion. House members were permitted

[8] Ibid., pp. 99–100.

[9] Glenn R. Parker and Roger H. Davidson, "Why Do Americans Love Their Congressmen So Much More than Their Congress?" *Legislative Studies Quarterly* 4 (1979):53–61.

[10] Roger H. Davidson and Walter J. Oleszek, *Congress and Its Members* (Washington, D.C.: Congressional Quarterly Press, 1981), p. 124.

TABLE 3.2
Personal Staffs of House and Senate Members,
1930–1979

Year	House Employees	Senate Employees
1930	870	280
1935	870	424
1947	1,440	590
1957	2,441	1,115
1967	4,055	1,749
1972	5,280	2,426
1977	6,942	3,554
1979	7,067	3,612

Source: John F. Bibby, Thomas E. Mann, and Norman J. Ornstein, *Vital Statistics on Congress, 1980*
(Washington, D.C.: American Enterprise Institute for
Public Policy Research, 1980), Table 5.2. Reprinted by
permission.

three reimbursed round-trips to the district in 1960. The number was subsequently increased to five (1966), twelve (1968),
eighteen (1973), twenty-six (1975), and finally to thirty-two
(1977).[11] Senators are currently permitted forty to forty-four
free round-trips to the state, depending on its size.

The growth of other official resources has kept pace. The most
important congressional perquisite is the franking privilege: the
right of members to use the mails free of charge for "official
business," which is broadly interpreted to include most kinds of
communications to constituents. Franked mail increased by
more than 600 percent between 1954 and 1970. A recent estimate put the total cost of congressional mail for a twelve-month
period (1976–1977) at more than $62 million, with an average
of more than $117,000 per member.[12] Not surprisingly, the vol-
ume of franked mail varies with the election cycle, as Figure 3.2
demonstrates; much more is sent out in months preceding an
election. Other media have not been overlooked. Facilities for

[11] Morris P. Fiorina, *Congress: Keystone of the Washington Establishment* (New Haven: Yale University Press, 1977), p. 61.
[12] *Hartford Courant,* March 28, 1977, p. 6.

FIGURE 3.2
Franked Mass Mailings by House Members, 1973–1978

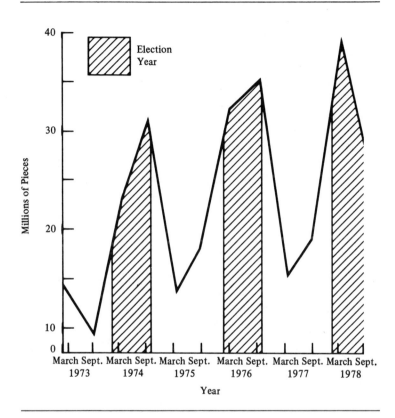

Source: Congressional Quarterly Weekly Report 38 (August 16, 1980), p. 2387. Copyright © 1980, Congressional Quarterly, Inc. Reprinted by permission.

preparing radio and television tapes and films are available to members free of charge. And in 1977, members voted themselves an unlimited WATS line for long distance telephone calls.

Plainly, one reason incumbents usually win reelection is that they work hard at it and control extensive resources that can be turned to electoral advantage. Mayhew suggested that the increasing electoral safety of House incumbents might be a straightforward consequence of more vigorous exploitation of

ever greater communications resources.[13] The accepted ideas
about voting behavior in congressional elections lent support to
this view. Voters were known to favor candidates with whom
they were familiar (that is, whose names they could recall when
asked), so the more extensive self-advertising by members of
Congress could be expected to have direct electoral payoffs,
assuming that it made them familiar to more voters. But appar-
ently it did not. John Ferejohn showed that the proportion of
voters who could recall incumbents' names did not increase between 1958 and 1970; nor did the incumbents' familiarity advantage over their challengers grow. He proposed that a change
in voting behavior was behind the enlarged incumbency advantage. Voters had become substantially less loyal to political parties during the 1960s and early 1970s. Perhaps they were merely
substituting one simple voting cue, incumbency, for another,
party.[14]

This explanation reflected a conception of voters as unin-
formed and superficial in their approach to voting decisions. As
Chapter 5 will show in greater detail, this view of congressional
voters has been rather extensively revised in light of more recent
research. And if, as it now appears, the congressional electorate
is more sophisticated and better informed than was once commonly thought, another explanation for the greater success of
House incumbents in recent years becomes more compelling.

Morris Fiorina argues that members of Congress have enhanced their own electoral fortunes not simply by advertising
themselves more extensively, but by changing the focus of their
activities and thus the content of the message they send to
voters. They have, in effect, created needs, then reaped the rewards of spending a larger part of their time serving them. Over
the past several decades, legislation enacted by Congress has
fostered an enormous increase in the size and scope of federal
government. This has generated an increasing volume of demands from citizens for help in coping with the bureaucratic
maze or in taking advantage of federal programs. Members
responded to the demand by continually adding to their capacity

[13] Mayhew, "Congressional Elections," p. 311.
[14] John A. Ferejohn, "On the Decline of Competition in Congressional
Elections," *American Political Science Review* 71 (1977):174.

TABLE 3.3
District Office Staffing, 1960–1974

Staffing Pattern	1960	1967	1974
Percentage of personal congressional staff assigned to district offices	14	26	34
Percentage of congressmen whose district offices are open only when the congressman is at home or after adjournment	29	11	2
Percentage of congressmen with multiple district offices	4	18	47

Source: Morris P. Fiorina, *Congress: Keystone of the Washington Establishment* (New Haven, Conn.: Yale University Press, 1977), p. 58. Copyright © 1977 by Yale University. Reprinted by permission of the publisher, Yale University Press.

to deliver assistance. The growth of personal staffs has already been noted. The use to which new staff resources have been put are equally significant. It is evident from Table 3.3 that a disproportionate share of additional personnel available to members has been used to augment their capacity to provide services to constituents.

The greater demand for services and the greater resources for providing them creates more opportunities for building credit with constituents. For electoral purposes, "the nice thing about case work is that it is mostly profit; one makes many more friends than enemies." [15] Case work is also nonpartisan. The party of the congressman delivering or the constituent receiving the assistance is irrelevant. What counts is the member's ability to deliver services, which increases with his tenure in Washington and his consequent seniority and familiarity with the administrative apparatus. It is therefore perfectly reasonable for voters to prefer candidates on the basis of their incumbency rather than on their party or policy positions. And it is equally reasonable for members to concentrate on providing services

[15] Morris P. Fiorina, "The Case of the Vanishing Marginals: The Bureaucracy Did It," *American Political Science Review* 71 (1977):180.

rather than making national policy as a means for staying in office.

Fiorina's thesis is still controversial,[16] but there is little question that attention to constituency service now commands an enlarged share of members' and their staffs' time. Newer members have been especially active in soliciting and responding to requests for assistance. One consequence is that first-term House members, once thought to be the most vulnerable incumbents, have become remarkably difficult to defeat. In 1974, for example, first-term House Republicans "as a group actually *improved* their position very slightly in the face of an exceptionally large national shift towards the Democrats." [17] In 1976, forty-eight of forty-nine Democrats who had been elected in 1974 to seats held by Republicans won a second term; seventy-two of seventy-four freshmen Democrats who sought reelection won. Not a single House Democrat first elected in 1978 was defeated in the Republican sweep of 1980.

The success of younger House members, who have "exhibited great ingenuity and phenomenal tenacity in 'cultivating' their districts," [18] suggests one important reason that the electoral value of incumbency is not a constant. It depends on what the incumbent does with the resources available, how hard he or she works to build and maintain support in the district. And this varies widely.[19]

It is safe to assume that incumbents who run for reelection

[16] See John R. Johannes and John C. McAdams, "The Congressional Incumbency Effect: Is It Casework, Policy Compatibility, or Something Else?"; Morris P. Fiorina, "Some Problems in Studying the Effects of Resource Allocation in Congressional Elections"; Diana Evans Yiannakis, "The Grateful Electorate: Casework and Congressional Elections"; and John C. McAdams and John R. Johannes, "Does Casework Matter? A Reply to Professor Fiorina," all in *American Journal of Political Science* 25 (1981):512–604.

[17] Walter Dean Burnham, "Insulation and Responsiveness in Congressional Elections," *Political Science Quarterly* 90 (1975):419.

[18] Charles M. Tidmarch, "The Second Time Around: Freshman Democratic House Members' 1976 Reelection Experiences" (Paper delivered during the Annual Meeting of the American Political Science Association, Washington, D.C., September 1–4, 1977), p. 27.

[19] For examples, see Alan L. Clem, ed., *The Making of Congressmen: Seven Campaigns of 1974* (North Scituate, Massachusetts: Duxbury Press, 1976).

want to stay in Congress. Why do some exploit the resources of office so much more vigorously than others to this end? The principal reason is that there are other important things to do with their time and energy and staff. Single-minded pursuit of reelection detracts from work in Washington and therefore from a member's power and influence in Congress. Reelection is an instrumental, not ultimate, goal. Some opportunities to build support back in the district must be foregone if a member is to share in governing the country. And the longer a member is in office, the more opportunities arise to influence policy and to gain the respect of others in government. Members very soon find that they have to balance their desire for electoral security against their desire for a successful career in Washington. This contributes a cyclical element to electoral careers that I will examine more fully later.

Discouraging the Opposition

Case work, trips back to the district, newsletters, and all the other things members do to promote reelection are not aimed merely at winning votes in the next election. They are also meant to influence the perceptions politically active people form of the member's hold on the district. The electoral value of incumbency lies not only in what it provides to the incumbent, but equally as well in how it affects the thinking of potential opponents and their potential supporters. Many incumbents win easily, by wide margins, because they face inexperienced, sometimes reluctant challengers, who lack the financial and organizational backing to mount a serious campaign for Congress. If an incumbent can convince potentially formidable opponents and people who control campaign resources that he is invincible, he is very likely to avoid a serious challenge and so will be invincible — as long as the impression holds.

This is so because politically skilled and ambitious nonincumbents follow rational career strategies; people who control campaign resources make strategically rational decisions about deploying them; and the volume of campaign resources at the disposal of a nonincumbent candidate has a great deal to do with how well he or she does at the polls.

Strategic Politicians

Other things equal, the strongest congressional candidates are those for whom politics is a career.[20] They have the most powerful motive and the greatest opportunity to master the craft of electoral politics. They are most likely to have experience in running campaigns and in holding elective office. They have the incentive and opportunity to build up contacts with other politically active and influential people and to put them under some obligation.

Ambitious career politicians also have the greatest incentive to follow a rational strategy for moving up the informal, but quite real, hierarchy of elective offices in the American political system. An experienced politician will have acquired important political assets — most typically, a lower elective office — that increase the probability of moving to a higher office. But these assets are at risk and may be lost if the attempt to advance fails. Thus the potentially strongest nonincumbent candidates will also make the most considered and cautious judgments about when to try for a congressional seat.[21]

Incumbency is central to their strategic calculations. Politically knowledgeable people are fully aware of the advantages of incumbency and of the long odds normally faced by challengers, and they adjust their behavior accordingly. Hence, for example, typically more than half of the candidates for open House seats have previously held an elective office, while such experienced candidates comprise less than a quarter of the candidates challenging incumbents. Within this large pattern, experienced challengers are more likely to run against incumbents who had closer contests in the last election; the average vote won by their party's candidate in the previous election is 40 percent, compared to 33 percent for inexperienced challengers. Table 3.4 presents the evidence for these points and reveals a clear pattern of strategic behavior among nonincumbent House candidates.

The career strategies of potential congressional candidates

[20] Gary C. Jacobson and Samuel Kernell, *Strategy and Choice in Congressional Elections* (New Haven: Yale University Press, 1981), chapter 3.
[21] Ibid., pp. 22–23.

TABLE 3.4
Strategic Behavior of Nonincumbent House Candidates, 1972–1980

	Percentage of Candidates Who Have Held Elective Office	
Year	Challengers	Open Seats
1972	21	47
1974	25	52
1976	22	60
1978	19	47
1980	26	59
Average, 1972–1980	23	53

	Average Percentage of Challenger's Party's Vote in Last Election	
Year	Challenger Who Has Held Elective Office	Challenger Who Has Not Held Elective Office
1972	40	33
1974	39	34
1976	40	33
1978	42	32
1980	40	34
Average, 1972–1980	40	33

Source: Data compiled by author.

are complimented and reinforced by those of individuals and groups that control campaign resources. The most important of these resources is money, although other forms of assistance can also be valuable. People and groups contribute to congressional campaigns for reasons ranging from selfless idealism to pure venality. But regardless of the purpose, most contribute more readily to nonincumbent candidates in campaigns that are expected to be close.[22] (The situation regarding incumbents is

[22] Gary C. Jacobson, *Money in Congressional Elections* (New Haven: Yale University Press, 1980), pp. 72–101.

somewhat different and will be considered later.) Resources are limited, and most contributors deploy them where they have the greatest chance of affecting the outcome; they try to avoid wasting money on a hopeless candidate. Solid evidence of this tendency is found in Table 3.5. In every election year for which the data are available, more money is contributed to candidates for open seats than to challengers, and more is contributed to challengers who face incumbents who had smaller margins of victory in the previous election (a simple measure of electoral vulnerability).

Thus expectations about the likelihood of electoral success influence the decisions of potential candidates and campaign contributors. The better the electoral odds, the stronger the can-

TABLE 3.5
Electoral Competition and Contributions to Nonincumbent House Candidates, 1972–1980 (in thousands of dollars)

	Challenger's Party's Vote in Last Election			
	Less than 40%	40% to 45%	45% to 50%	Open Seats
1972				
Democrats	15	37	67	97
Republicans	24	38	66	91
1974				
Democrats	44	68	96	103
Republicans	13	32	41	80
1976				
Democrats	29	36	70	144
Republicans	23	85	126	98
1978				
Democrats	42	68	146	213
Republicans	36	86	220	193
1980				
Democrats	47	79	152	189
Republicans	81	153	232	204

Sources: 1972 and 1974: Common Cause; 1976 and 1978: Federal Election Commission; 1980: Alan Ehrenhalt, ed., Politics in America: Members of Congress in Washington and at Home (Washington, D.C.: Congressional Quarterly, 1981).

didate who runs and the more money contributed to his campaign. Furthermore, strong candidates themselves attract campaign money, and the availability of campaign money attracts strong candidates. A system of mutually reinforcing decisions and expectations thus links nonincumbent candidates and contributors with each other and with perceived electoral conditions.

Money in Congressional Elections

Nonincumbent candidates are wise, indeed, to worry about the availability of money for the campaign. For how well they do on election day is a direct function of how much campaign money they raise and spend. In every election year since 1972 (when the first reasonably accurate campaign finance data were gathered), statistical analysis has shown that how much money a nonincumbent candidate spends has a large effect on the proportion of votes he receives. The connection is particularly strong for candidates challenging incumbents. And it remains strong even when the effects of other variables, such as the strength of the party in the district or national electoral tides, are controlled. Furthermore, it is not weakened when the possibility of reverse causation — (expected) votes generating contributions, rather than campaign spending generating votes — is taken into account.[23]

The exact amount of money a nonincumbent candidate needs to run a competitive campaign cannot, of course, be precisely determined. It varies from district to district and from state to state, depending on the structure and cost of mass media advertising, the vigor of local parties and other politically active organizations, and local campaign styles. And it increases every election year; campaign costs have even outstripped inflation in recent years.[24] But it is safe to say that an average competitive

[23] Ibid., pp. 136–145.

[24] See F. Christopher Arterton, Gary C. Jacobson, Xandra Kayden, and Gary Orren, *An Analysis of the Impact of the Federal Election Campaign Act, 1972–1978*, a Report by the Campaign Finance Study Group to the Committee on House Administration of the U.S. House of Representatives (Institute of Politics, John F. Kennedy School of Government, Harvard University, May 1979).

House campaign now costs well over $200,000, and a serious Senate campaign can cost more than ten times as much in a large state like California, New York, or Texas. In the elections of the 1970s, a reasonable figure for the cost of a competitive campaign — one which does not guarantee victory, but at least does not preclude it — was consistently more than twice as much as the typical challenger was able to spend in each election year. Candidates for open seats did notably better, as the figures in Table 3.5 indicate. Their average spending is certainly within the range of the cost of a serious campaign; these were often close, hard-fought elections.

Defeating an incumbent is expensive, and relatively few challengers have been able to raise enough funds to be serious threats. But those who do acquire sufficient resources can make incumbents feel anything but safe. For incumbents, spending a great deal of money on the campaign is a sign of weakness rather than strength. In fact, the more money they spend on the campaign, the worse they do on election day. Spending money does not cost them votes, to be sure; rather, incumbents raise and spend more money the more strongly they feel themselves challenged. The more their opponent spends, the more they spend. But campaign spending by incumbents is *not* related to how well they do at the polls once the challenger's spending is taken into account. The marginal return on campaign expenditures (in the form of votes) is much greater for challengers than for incumbents. Therefore, the more spent by both the challenger and the incumbent, the greater the challenger's share of the vote.[25]

Campaign spending has different effects for incumbents and nonincumbents because campaigning is subject to diminishing returns. Congressional incumbents usually exploit their official resources for reaching constituents so thoroughly that the additional increment of information about their virtues put forth in the campaign adds little or nothing to what is already known and felt about them. As you shall see in Chapter 5, how well voters know and like incumbents is completely unrelated to how much they spend on the campaign. The situation is quite different for nonincumbents. Most are obscure before the cam-

[25] See Jacobson, *Money,* pp. 42–43.

paign, and the extent to which they penetrate the awareness of voters — which is crucial to winning votes — is directly related to how extensively they campaign. The money spent on nonincumbents' campaigns buys the attention and recognition that incumbents already enjoy at the outset of the campaign.

Incumbents also face quite different fundraising problems than do challengers and other nonincumbents. Many interest groups contribute to campaigns not so much to influence the outcome as to gain influence with, or at least access to, people who are likely to be in a position to help or hurt them. They certainly waste no money on sure losers, but they will have no qualms about giving money to sure winners even when it is not really needed for the campaign. Whether or not incumbents tap this source of funds depends on whether or not they think they need the money. Members of Congress almost uniformly loathe asking for contributions and will avoid doing so if they do not feel the need for it (given the strength of the opposition they are facing). But if they are threatened, they have sources to tap that are not nearly so readily available to challengers. Even parties and ideological interest groups rally to support threatened incumbents of the preferred party or ideology; it is easier to hold on to a seat than to take one from the opposition.

Incumbents, then, can generally raise as much campaign money as they think they need. But spending the money does them comparatively little good. What really matters is the amount spent by the challenger (and, related to it, how qualified and skilled he or she is). This means that *the incumbent's most effective electoral strategy is to discourage serious opposition.* The most effective way to do this is to avoid showing any signs of electoral vulnerability. Even the most implacable political enemies will not mobilize the full range of their political resources against the incumbent if they see no chance of success. Maintaining an active presence in the district helps discourage the opposition. So does working to keep the electoral coalition that put the member into office in the first place in good repair. Since elections are the most solid source of information on a member's electoral strength, it is particularly important to avoid slippage at the polls. An unexpectedly weak showing in one election inspires even stronger opposition in the next. As one incumbent put it, "it is important for me to keep the young state representatives and city councilmen away. If they have the feeling that I'm invincible, they won't try. That reputation is very intangible. [But] your vote margin is part of it." [26]

It is also shrewd strategy for incumbents to diminish the *intensity* of opposition in the district. No one can please everyone, and nothing is to be gained by alienating one's own supporters. But occasional friendly gestures to potentially hostile political forces may be sufficient to dampen their enthusiasm for organizing an all-out campaign against the member.

From an incumbent's perspective, then, elections are not merely discrete hurdles to be cleared at regular two-year intervals. They are, as Richard F. Fenno, Jr.'s unique research has shown, a series of connected events that form part of a "career in the district" (which is simultaneous with the career in Washington).[27] Winning is always crucial, of course. But winning in a way that minimizes future opposition is just as desirable in the long run.

Other important insights into congressional election processes emerge from thinking in terms of congressional careers rather than single elections. Fenno discovered that House members' careers in the district passed through identifiable stages. In the first, expansionist phase, members devote a great deal of time and energy to building up their base of consistent supporters. Beginning with a core of solid backers, they work to reach additional individuals and groups in the district they hope to incorporate into their electoral coalition. The expansionist phase begins before the first election and continues for at least a few more. The capacity of freshman members to increase their electoral margins even in the face of strong contrary electoral tides is a sign of this effort and of its efficacy.

At some point, after a few elections, members typically enter into a protectionist career phase, in which they work to maintain the support they have built up over the years, but no longer attempt to add to it. By this time they have often discouraged serious opposition by a show of growing electoral strength. And

---

[26] Quoted in Richard F. Fenno, Jr., *Home Style: House Members in Their Districts* (Boston: Little, Brown, 1978), p. 13.
[27] Ibid., chapter 6.

they have been in Washington long enough to have acquired some influence and responsibility. Working the district becomes a less attractive alternative to making policy and exercising legislative skills. It is at this stage that members risk "losing touch with the district," to use the politicians' cliche. If they do, they become electorally vulnerable. But their vulnerability may not become apparent at all until it is tested.

This pattern of congressional career development strongly affects the efficacy of strategies pursued by nonincumbents seeking congressional seats. The best opportunity arises when the incumbent dies or retires, and it is not uncommon to find ambitious young politicians biding their time until a seat becomes open, after which a lively scramble ensues among them for the nomination and election.[28] First-term members also attract unusually vigorous opposition. The strategic thinking this represents makes apparent sense; newly elected members do not have as firm a hold on their districts as they will develop later, so the challenge may seem a question of now or never. Politicians who use electoral margins as evidence of electoral vulnerability will focus on these new incumbents because a disproportionate share of them first win office in close elections. But as we have already observed, first-term incumbents have been especially difficult to defeat in recent years. So this strategy, though plausible, is misdirected.

Incumbents should obviously be most vulnerable in the protectionist stage of their careers. Electoral support is not won once and for all. It requires continual renewal and reinforcement. Members who work merely to maintain their base of support may actually let it slip, especially if they enjoy a few elections with feeble opposition that disguises any weakening of their hold on the district. A challenger who, through luck or cleverness, puts together a serious campaign against a member whose hold on the district has imperceptibly atrophied may surprise everyone, the incumbent and himself included. An example is Duncan Hunter, who defeated Democratic incumbent Lionel Van Deerlin in the 1980 contest for the 42nd District of California. Van Deerlin had not been seriously challenged in

[28] See Harvey L. Schantz, "Contested and Uncontested Primaries for the U.S. House," *Legislative Studies Quarterly* 5 (1980):550.

years; he was unaware of his own electoral weakness and of the progress his opponent was making until it was too late to do anything about it. Hunter had decided to run only at the last minute and then on the theory that, although he was likely to lose, he would be in a stronger position to take the seat in 1982, especially if, as many anticipated, Van Deerlin retired. Hunter's hesitation did not prevent a vigorous and well-financed campaign, and he wound up with 53 percent of the vote, compared to the 24 percent won by the token Republican challenger in 1978 — a shift of 29 percentage points between the two elections. Van Deerlin was only the most surprised of a number of senior House Democrats in 1980. Republican challengers were unable to win any seats from first-term Democrats but defeated fourteen incumbents who had served at least ten years, eight who had had served at least eighteen years.[29]

This example says something important about the "safety" of incumbents. Winning is by no means a sure thing in any individual case as it might appear from the aggregate statistics on incumbent reelection rates and margins. As David Mayhew put it, "When we say 'Congressman Smith is unbeatable,' we do not mean that there is nothing he could do that would lose him his seat. Rather we mean, 'Congressman Smith is unbeatable as long as he continues to do the things he is doing.' " [30] The few examples each election year of supposedly secure incumbents going down to defeat are sufficient lessons to the rest; they make most incumbents remarkably responsive to changing political forces. How this affects their performance in Washington, and the performance of Congress as an institution, will be taken up in Chapters 7 and 8.

Since most incumbents do work hard to remain in office and are therefore extremely difficult to defeat, it is not absurd to ask why, under most circumstances, anyone challenges them at all. Part of the answer is that a fair proportion of incumbents are *not* challenged. In 1978, for example, 16 percent of the House incumbents had no general election opposition; 12 per-

---

[29] Michael Barone and Grant Ujifusa, *The Alamanac of American Politics 1982* (Washington, D.C.: Barone and Company, 1981), pp. 158–159.

[30] Mayhew, *Electoral Connection,* p. 37.

cent were unopposed in both the primary and general election.[31] But most are challenged, even those who appear to be unbeatable; why?

One reason is the naivete of the challenger. As David Leuthold noted in his study of San Francisco area congressional campaigns, "inexperienced candidates often did not realize that they had no chance of winning." [32] Most challengers recognize that the odds are against them, of course. But their hopes may be buoyed by the inherent uncertainties of electoral politics and a large dose of self-deception. Writing from personal experience — he is a political scientist who ran for Congress but did not get past the primary — Sandy Maisel points out that "politicians tend to have an incredible ability to delude themselves" about their electoral prospects.[33] Maisel's report of his own and other congressional primaries in 1978 provides several additional insights into the question. Many congressional candidates had planned for years to run for Congress — some day. The only question was when; and when circumstances seem only a little bit more favorable than usual, their thinking was, "if not now, when?" Or, more desperately, "now or never." [34]

Candidates can delude themselves all the more easily because they do not have the resources to find out just how difficult their task is; they cannot afford a top quality poll that would tell them where they stand with the electorate and what they would have to achieve to win the election. They most often rely instead on their own political intuition and, to a lesser degree, on the opinions of local political leaders.[35] Both are inclined to tell them what they want to hear, so it is not difficult for them to overestimate their chances.

Even candidates who are certain they will not win find motives for running. The most common reason given is to provide

[31] Calculated from L. Sandy Maisel, "From Obscurity to Oblivion: Congressional Primary Elections in 1978," manuscript, Colby College, Table 1.1.

[32] David A. Leuthold, *Electioneering in a Democracy: Campaigns for Congress* (New York: John Wiley, 1968), p. 22.

[33] Maisel, "Congressional Primary Elections," p. 31.

[34] Ibid., pp. 20–21.

[35] Ibid., Table 2-2.

some opposition, to make sure the party is represented on the ballot, "to demonstrate that the party had a spark of life in the district." [36] Party leaders may run themselves when they are unable to find anyone else willing to face a drubbing.[37] Some run to build for their own or the party's future, as did many southern Republicans in the 1950s and early 1960s. Others evidently run in order to advertise themselves in their professions; this reason is not often volunteered, but a remarkable proportion of young attorneys, insurance agents, and real estate dealers turn up as challengers in districts where they have little hope of winning.[38]

Challengers who are naive, inexperienced, self-deceiving, or running without hope of winning do not make particularly formidable opponents. Incumbents blessed with such opposition are reelected with ease. But every so often one is rudely surprised, for uncertainty is an inevitable component of congressional election politics. More about that in the next chapter.

[36] Robert J. Huckshorn and Robert C. Spencer, *The Politics of Defeat* (Amherst, Massachusetts: University of Massachusetts Press, 1971), p. 75.

[37] See John F. Bibby, "The Case of the Young Old Pro: The Sixth District of Wisconsin," *Making of Congressmen*, p. 216, for an example.

[38] I am finding this to be the case in an ongoing research project examining the backgrounds of House challengers since 1946.

4
Congressional Campaigns

It should be apparent by now that much of the action in congressional election politics takes place outside the formal campaigns and election periods. But this in no way implies that campaigns are inconsequential. The bottom line is that votes have to be sought, and the most concentrated work to win them takes place through the campaign. The formal campaign is of course crucial to those candidates, including most nonincumbents, who have not been able to match the more or less incessant campaigning now typical of congressional incumbents.

Election campaigns have a simple dominant goal: to win at least a plurality of votes cast, thus the election. Little else is simple about them, however. Campaigns confront candidates with difficult problems of analysis and execution which even in the best of circumstances are only imperfectly mastered.

The analytical work required for an effective congressional campaign is suggested by the variety of campaign contexts set forth in Chapter 2. States and districts are not homogeneous lumps; voters do not form an undifferentiated mass. They are divided by boundaries of community, class, race, politics, and geography. Candidates (and those who help them put campaigns together) need to recognize these boundaries and understand their implications for building winning coalitions. Often those without political experience do not, and this in itself guarantees failure.[1]

The basic questions are straightforward: Which constituents are likely to become solid supporters? Who might be persuaded? Which groups are best written off as hopeless? How can potential supporters be reached? What kinds of appeals are likely to prove effective? All of these questions must be answered twice, and in different ways, if there is a primary election. They cannot be addressed at all without some cognitive handle on the constituency; campaigners are inevitably theorists.

Successful campaigners recognize this need, at least implicitly. Members of the House develop highly differentiated images of their constituencies. Their behavior is guided by a coherent diagnosis of district components and forces. Knowledge is grounded in experience; they learn at least as much about their constituents from campaigning and from visiting the district between elections as their constituents learn about them. This kind of learning takes time, and its necessity is another reason for viewing House elections from a time perspective longer than a campaign period or a two-year term.[2] It is also one source of the incumbency advantage and helps to explain why politically experienced nonincumbents make superior House candidates.

The analytic tasks facing Senate candidates are, in most states, substantially more formidable than those facing House candidates. They normally deal with much more heterogeneous constituencies scattered over much wider areas. Incumbents as well as challengers usually suffer far more uncertainty regarding ways in which political elements may be combined into winning coalitions. Few have the opportunity to know their states as intimately as House candidates may know their districts.

The deepest understanding of the political texture of a state or district will not, by itself, win elections. Effective campaigns

---

[1] See Linda L. Fowler, "Candidate Perceptions of Electoral Coalitions: Limits and Possibilities" (Paper delivered during the Conference on Congressional Elections, Rice University and the University of Houston, Houston, Texas, January 10–12, 1980).

[2] Richard F. Fenno, Jr., *Home Style: House Members in Their Districts* (Boston: Little, Brown, 1978), pp. 171–172.

require a strategy for gathering at least a plurality of votes and the means to carry out that strategy. The central problem is communication. As the next chapter will show, what voters know about candidates has a strong effect on how they decide to vote. Voters who have no information about a candidate are much less likely to vote for him than those who do. The *content* of the information is also consequential, to be sure, but no matter how impressive the candidate or persuasive the message, it will not help if potential voters remain unaware of them.

Two resources are necessary to communicate with voters: money and organization. They may be combined in different ways, but overcoming serious opposition requires adequate supplies of both. Money is crucial because it buys access to the media of communication: radio, television, newspapers, direct mail, pamphlets, billboards, bumperstickers, bullhorns, and so on. Organization is necessary to raise money, to schedule the candidate's use of his personal time and energy to reach voters and more active supporters efficiently, and to help get out the vote on election day.

Campaign Money

Raising money is, by consensus, the most unpleasant part of a campaign. Many candidates find it demeaning to ask people for money and are uncomfortable with the implications of accepting it.[3] But most do it, because they cannot get elected without it. Congressional campaign finances are regulated by the Federal Election Campaign Act (FECA) and its amendments, enforced by the Federal Election Commission. The law requires full disclosure of the sources of campaign contributions and also restricts the amount of money that parties, groups, and individuals may give to congressional candidates.[4] Since its enactment in 1971, fundraising has become somewhat more difficult; but we know much more about it.

[3] Gary C. Jacobson, *Money in Congressional Elections* (New Haven: Yale University Press, 1980), pp. 67, 170–171.

[4] Individuals may give no more than $1,000 per candidate per campaign (primary and general election campaigns are considered separate) up to a total of $20,000 in an election year; nonparty political action committees may give no more than $5,000 per candidate per campaign; party contribution limits are discussed later in this chapter.

Aggregate figures on the sources of money for House and Senate campaigns in the last five elections are presented in Table 4.1. The greatest share of campaign money is contributed by private individuals, typically about 60 percent in House elections, about 70 percent in Senate elections. Nonparty committees are the second most important source of campaign funds, and their share has been growing steadily, from 14 percent in 1972 to 26 percent in 1980. This category includes all political action committees (PACs) organized by unions, corporations, trade and professional associations, and ideological and issue-oriented groups of many kinds.

Business-oriented PACs are the fastest growing source of PAC money by far, as the data in Table 4.2 show clearly. Corporate PAC contributions surpassed those of labor organizations for the first time in 1980; they also have the greatest potential for further growth, since only a small percentage of business corporations have as yet set up PACs.[5] Labor's relative importance as a source of campaign funds for congressional candidates has steadily diminished. The implications of this decline are disturbing to union leaders and to many Democrats. Although business PACs did not, at first, favor Republican candidates disproportionately, this happened only because they favored incumbents and most incumbents — and all committee and subcommittee chairmen — were Democrats. In the last two elections, these groups have given a larger share of their funds to Republicans, whom they usually find to be more congenial ideologically. The distribution of PAC contributions to 1980 candidates by party and incumbency status is shown in Table 4.3. Corporate PACs favor Republicans decisively; labor PACs prefer Democrats overwhelmingly. All but "unconnected organizations" — mostly ideological groups — give two-thirds of their funds to incumbents. If corporate PACs continue to grow in importance and if their preference for Republicans becomes even more pronounced, Democrats can expect to be at a serious financial disadvantage. They will be even worse off if they lose control of the House as they have of the Senate. Efforts made in

[5] Edwin M. Epstein, "The Rise of Political Action Committees" (Colloquium paper, Woodrow Wilson International Center for Scholars, June 15, 1978), p. 76.

TABLE 4.1

Sources of Campaign Contributions to House and Senate Candidates, 1972–1980

Elections	1972	1974	1976	1978	1980
House					
Average contributions	$51,752 [a]	$61,084	$79,421	$111,232	$148,268
Percentage of contributions from:					
Individuals	60 [b]	73	59	61	67 [b]
Parties	17	4	8	5	4
Nonparty committees	14	17	23	25	29
Candidates [c]	—	6	9	9	—
Unknown	9	—	—	—	—
Senate					
Average contributions	$353,933 [a]	$455,515	$624,094	$951,390	$1,079,346
Percentage of contributions from:					
Individuals	67	76	69	70	78 [b]
Parties	14	6	4	6	2
Nonparty committees	12	11	15	13	21
Candidates [c]	0.4	1	12	8	—
Unknown	8	6	—	—	—

[a] Some contributions before April 7, 1972, may have gone unreported.
[b] Includes candidates' contributions to their own campaigns.
[c] Includes candidates' loans unrepaid at time of filing.

Source: Compiled by author from data supplied by Common Cause (1972 and 1974) and the Federal Election Commission (1976–1980).

TABLE 4.2
The Growth of PAC Contributions to Congressional Candidates, 1974–1980

Type of PAC Contribution:	Contributions (in millions)				
	1974	1976	1978	1980	1974–1980
Labor	$6.3 (50)*	$8.2 (36)	$10.3 (29)	$13.1 (24)	24
Corporate	2.5 (20)	7.1 (31)	9.8 (28)	19.2 (35)	359
Trade/Membership/Health	2.3 (18)	4.5 (20)	11.5 (33)	16.1 (29)	319
Other	1.4 (11)	2.8 (12)	3.5 (10)	6.9 (12)	195
Total PAC Contributions	12.5	22.6	35.1	55.3	
Adjusted for Inflation (1980 = 100)	20.9	32.7	44.3	55.3	

	Percent Change (adjusted for inflation)			
	1974–1976	1976–1978	1978–1980	1974–1980
Type of PAC Contribution:				
Labor	13	7	0	24
Corporate	146	17	55	359
Trade/Membership/Health	169	117	11	319
Other	73	6	56	195
Total PAC Contributions	57	32	24	164

* Percentage of all PAC contributions; numbers may not sum to 100 because of rounding.
Source: Federal Election Commission data.

54

TABLE 4.3
PAC Contributions to Congressional Candidates, 1979–1980
(in millions of dollars)

	Total Contributions	Party Affiliation	
		Democrats	Republicans
Type of PAC:			
Labor	$13.1	$12.2	$ 0.9
Corporate	19.2	6.9	12.2
Trade/Membership/Health	16.1	7.1	9.0
Other	6.9	2.8	4.1
Total	55.3	29.0	26.2

	Candidate Status		
	Incumbents	Challengers	Open Seats
Type of PAC:			
Labor	$ 9.3	$ 2.2	$ 1.6
Corporate	11.0	5.8	2.4
Trade/Membership/Health	10.3	3.7	2.1
Other	3.1	2.6	1.2
Total	33.8	14.3	7.2

Note: Figures under *Party Affiliation* and *Candidate Status* do not always
equal the total contribution due to rounding.
Source: Federal Election Commission data.

the 95th Congress to limit how much money candidates could
accept from PACs were designed to protect Democrats from this
threat, but they were not successful.[6]

Political parties are a much less important source of *direct*
campaign contributions, and their share of donations to candidates has been on the decline. These figures underline the fact
that candidates are largely on their own when it comes to financing the campaign directly; parties provide little of the where-

[6] Jacobson, *Money,* pp. 238–241.

withall. But these data understate the contribution of parties — particularly the Republican — to congressional campaigns because they do not include the "in-kind" assistance that party committees are allowed to give to candidates.

Direct party contributions are limited to $5,000 per candidate per election for House candidates. This means that any party committee can give, at most, $10,000 to a candidate in an election year ($15,000 if there is a runoff primary). But both the national committees and the national congressional campaign committees of each party can contribute this amount, so direct national party contributions can amount to $20,000 in House elections, roughly 10 percent of what it costs to mount a minimally serious challenge. In addition, parties may make coordinated expenditures on behalf of House candidates, the amount being adjusted for inflation; for 1980, it was $14,720. In 1980, then, national party committees could put as much as $34,720 into a House race, a considerable amount of money, but less than 20 percent of what it is likely to cost to threaten an incumbent.

Much more can be put into Senate contests. Direct party contributions are limited to a maximum of $17,500 per candidate for all national committees. But the limits on coordinated expenditures are much higher and can be effectively doubled by a clever legal device. The 1980 limits on coordinated expenditures in Senate races were two cents times the voting age population, adjusted for inflation since 1974, or $29,440, whichever is greater. Fourteen states had $29,440 ceilings; California, the most populous state, had a coordinated spending ceiling of $485,024. State parties may also spend two cents per voting age resident on behalf of Senate candidates, but few of them have the money to do it. Republican leaders adopted an interpretation of the law that allows national committees to pick up the state party's share if the state party agrees to let the national party act as its agent. They entered into agency agreements with thirty-three of the thirty-four states with Senate elections in 1980, leaving out only Indiana, where the state party did not need the help. The legality of this ploy was challenged by the Democrats; they lost their case before the Supreme Court in 1981. Meanwhile, it was allowed for the 1980 elections. Republican national party committees could thus spend as much as $987,548 on a Senate candidate (twice $485,024, plus $17,500, in California); the lowest limit was $76,380.[7] This amounts to a much larger proportion of the money needed to finance a full-scale campaign than can be supplied to House candidates.

Coordinated expenditures can be made for almost any campaign activity. The only condition is that the party as well as the candidate have some control over how the money is spent. National parties typically foot the bill for conducting polls, producing campaign ads, and buying media time — major expenses in areas where technical expertise is essential. These services are most useful in Senate campaigns, and the law allows the greatest party activity in these contests, so most coordinated spending by both parties takes place in Senate campaigns. It is no coincidence that Republicans were so much more successful in Senate than in House campaigns in 1980, though other complimentary forces were obviously involved.

The injection of more than nine million dollars of national party money into congressional elections through coordinated spending represents a striking departure from past congressional campaign finance practices. Formerly, parties were most active in congressional campaigns at the state and local level. The decline of these party units and their separation from congressional campaigns helped foster the system of personal, independent campaigning now typical of congressional candidates. Parties at the national level focused on presidential elections, making only the most limited attempts to intervene in other federal elections. The Republicans (soon, it appears, to be imitated by the Democrats) have altered this pattern radically. The change is so recent that its ramifications are not yet clear. But it does have the potential to reverse the trend toward independence and fragmentation in the conduct of campaigns and, as a result, activity in Congress. It is the subject of further speculation in Chapter 8.

The final source of campaign money is the candidate's own pocket. The Supreme Court's decision in *Buckley* v. *Valeo* (96 S. Ct. 612) overturned limits on how much of his or her own money a candidate may spend to get elected, which gives no small advantage to wealthy candidates. An example is Senator

[7] Larry Light, "Republican Groups Dominate in Party Campaign Spending," *Congressional Quarterly Weekly Report* 38 (November 1, 1980): 3234–3236.

H. John Heinz of Pennsylvania, heir to the pickle and catsup fortune, who spent $2,465,500 of his own money to finance his 1976 campaign.[8] His opponent could legally accept contributions no larger than $1,000 from individuals and $5,000 from PACs for the general election (the same limits apply for a primary campaign). The most fortunate candidates are those who can loan their campaigns substantial sums of money, then have the debt repaid from other sources once they have won the election (and thus can raise money from people who are now anxious to be their friends).

The most important aspect of fundraising is convincing potential donors that their money will not be wasted. This requires convincing them that the candidate has a plausible chance of winning and that he will be more attentive to their values and interests than will his opponent. Techniques of persuasion range from polls and old election returns to a smooth tongue backed by a lively imagination, from recitation of a political record to solemn promises. Large contributions must usually be solicited face-to-face by the candidate himself or a prominent, high-status fundraiser. Smaller contributions are sought at meetings, rallies, or, increasingly, through direct mail appeals sent to individuals at home. The growing popularity of this last method has become the source of some concern, since direct mail pleas are most successful when they play on strong emotions, anger or fear, to convince people to support the candidate. More extreme candidates or issue positions are thus favored.[9]

However the money is acquired, timing is crucial. It is as important to have money available when it is needed as it is to have it in the first place. In general, money available early in the campaign is put to much better use than money received later. Early money is seed money for the entire campaign effort; it is needed to organize, plan, and raise more money. This circumstance adds to the advantage of personal wealth and also enhances the importance of national party and other organiza-

[8] Jacobson, *Money*, p. 100.
[9] Xandra Kayden, "The Nationalizing of the Party System," in *Parties, Interest Groups, and Campaign Finance Laws,* ed. Michael J. Malbin (Washington, D.C.: American Enterprise Institute for Public Policy Research, 1980), p. 266.

tions that are willing to make contributions and provide help early in the campaign.

Campaign Organizations

Campaign organizations usually have to be built from scratch for each election, making seed money particularly crucial. There was a time when, in many places, vigorous party organizations operated on a permanent basis and worked for entire party tickets. This is rarely the case now. Even when parties were robust, congressional candidates were not the centers of attention, for local parties were interested primarily in patronage, and congressmen controlled little of that. Now that party organizations have withered, congressional candidates are usually very much on their own when it comes to mounting a campaign. Fenno found from his observation of eighteen congressmen that

> in only two or three cases is there an integrated working relationship between the congressman's personal organization and the local party organization. That is exactly the way most of our House members want it — separate organizations pursuing separate tasks. The task of the congressman's personal organization is to keep him in Congress. The task of the local party organization is to keep the party in control of local offices.[10]

Congressional campaign organizations are personal, temporary, and, for the most part, staffed with volunteers. Each of these characteristics affects how organizations perform their basic mission of building a field operation and raising money. Because they are ephemeral and must rely on people giving their time and energy without pay, a great deal of effort goes into internal organizational maintenance. Xandra Kayden observed that "most of the campaign staff devotes most of its time to creating and maintaining the campaign organization." [11] Campaign organizations cannot be hierarchical because sanctions are so few.

[10] Fenno, *Home Style*, p. 113.
[11] Xandra Kayden, *Campaign Organization* (Lexington, Massachusetts: D.C. Heath, 1978), p. 61.

They cannot "learn" from their mistakes because they exist for such a short time and go out of business at the very time the real effectiveness of their work is measured — on election day. To be sure, candidates who conduct more than one campaign — notably, incumbents — gain useful experience and develop a core of experienced campaign workers who can be called on in the future; this is another thing that strengthens their candidacies. But organizations usually still have to be put together anew each time, and each contest presents unique problems.

One straightforward way of coping with the task of creating a campaign organization is to buy one. As parties atrophied, professional campaign specialists took over many of their functions and pioneered a variety of new electoral techniques adapted to an age of television and computers. It is possible for a candidate to hire an outfit that will handle the entire campaign.[12] But professionals are expensive. Many House candidates cannot afford them and so do without campaign professionals even as consultants.[13] Senate candidates, with larger campaigns and bigger budgets, are more likely to make use of their services.

There are signs that parties are adjusting to the contemporary political environment by transforming themselves into centers of technical expertise of the kind found in professional campaign organizations. As noted before, Republicans at the national level have been particularly active in developing the means to provide their candidates with valuable technical assistance. Some state parties have also moved in this direction.[14] But despite such developments, most congressional candidates remain largely on their own.

Short of buying one, the only way most congressional candidates can have an adequate campaign organization is to build one themselves. Close political friends, the "personal constituency" that Fenno noticed all his congressmen had acquired, form

[12] See Section 2 of Robert Agranoff, ed., *The New Style in Election Campaigns*, 2nd ed. (Boston: Holbrook Press, 1976), for an idea of what is possible.

[13] Decision Making Information and Hart Research Associates, *A Study of the Impact of the Federal Election Campaign Act on the 1976 Elections* (Study prepared for the Federal Election Commission, 1977), p. 103.

[14] Robert Agranoff, "The Role of Political Parties in the New Campaigning," *New Style in Campaigns*, pp. 123–141.

the core. Other components are added as they are available. Some Democrats, for example, receive organizational assistance from labor unions. Fragments of local parties can sometimes be used. Inner city Black candidates may work through neighborhood churches. In recent years, single-issue groups, such as those opposing the Vietnam War or abortion, have provided organizational help to supporters of their cause. Almost any existing group with political interests can be absorbed into a campaign organization. In the 13th District of Florida, condominium associates are politically important because "the large condominiums have brought together into one easily accessible location many articulate people with a desire to become involved in local politics." [15] The kind of organization a candidate assembles depends on what kinds of groups are available, which ones he can appeal to, his range of contacts, his resources, and his degree of political skill.

Campaign Strategies

In a broad sense, everyone knows what campaigns are supposed to do: find and expand the pool of citizens favoring the candidate, and get them to the polls on election day. Just how best to do it is another matter. As one political veteran told John Kingdon, "I don't know very much about elections. I've been in a lot of them." [16] In fact, the central motif of almost every discussion of campaign strategy is *uncertainty*.

What is the most efficient way to reach voters? No one knows for sure. The most frequently expressed sentiment is that "half the money spent on campaigns is wasted. The trouble is, we don't know which half." [17] The effects of uncertainty about what works and what does not pervade campaign decision making. Successful candidates are inclined to do what they did in the past; they must have done something right, even if they cannot

---

[15] Michael Barone, Grant Ujifusa, and Douglas Matthews, *The Almanac of American Politics 1980: The Senators, the Representatives, the Governors — Their Records, States, and Districts* (New York: E.P. Dutton, 1979), p. 194.

[16] John W. Kingdon, *Candidates for Office: Beliefs and Strategies* (New York: Random House, 1968), p. 87.

[17] One of Fenno's congressmen raised it to 75 percent; see Fenno, *Home Style*, p. 17.

be sure what; a degree of superstition is understandable. Other candidates also follow tradition. Kayden concludes that "basically, campaigns produce literature because campaigns have always produced literature." [18] The same may be said of yard signs, bumperstickers, and campaign buttons. They appear in every election year not so much because they have ever been shown to be effective, but because everyone expects them and their absence would be noticed, if only by the campaign's activists (hence they may be part of organizational maintenance).

On the other hand, uncertainty also invites innovation. Challengers, underdogs, and former losers have an incentive to try new tactics. For example, Lawton Chiles won a surprise victory in the 1970 Florida senate election by walking the length of Florida, talking and listening to people along the way. Other candidates quickly imitated him. While it was still fresh, the tactic generated abundant free publicity and far more attention than Chiles and the other candidates could have afforded to buy. Similarly, Tom Harkin, challenging the Republican incumbent for Iowa's 5th District in 1972, made news by working for a day at a time in a variety of blue-collar jobs, ostensibly to get close to the common experience. Others soon picked up the idea. Whatever seems to work is imitated by others, so the novelty and therefore effectiveness of such tactics fade. But there is always something new. In 1980, Kenneth Snider, Democratic challenger in Indiana's 8th District, dropped in on voters with the helicopter he had purchased especially for the campaign; the news media loved it.[19] Snider lost the election, but won a respectable 45 percent of the vote.

Two groups of activities are common to all full-scale campaigns. One is mass media advertising. The candidate's name and perhaps a short message are presented to the voters via some combination of television, radio, newspaper advertisements, billboards, or mass mailings. The choice of media is partly strategic and partly dictated by cost and available resources. Most House campaigns, for example, do not use paid television. In large

---

[18] Kayden, *Campaign Organization*, p. 120.
[19] "The Outlook: Senate, House and Governors," *Congressional Quarterly Weekly Report* 38 (October 11, 1980):3014, 3017.

metropolitan areas it is inefficient and far too expensive for candidates without extraordinarily ample funds. Candidates must pay for the audience they reach; at the extreme (greater New York City), constituents may comprise less than 5 percent of the audience. Still, House candidates with enough money do use television advertising even if it is very wasteful, for even so, it may be the only way to reach many of the voters.

Senate campaigns are usually able to use television much more efficiently because constituencies are entire states. This helps candidates who are not already well known, hence challengers, and can be added to the list of factors that make Senate campaigns so much more competitive, on the average, than House campaigns.

Regardless of which combination of media is chosen, the basic goal is to get the candidate's name before the public. Though little else about mass communication may be certain, it is well established that mass media coverage is positively related to public awareness of people, products, or events. As we shall see in the next chapter, the more nonincumbent candidates spend on a campaign, the more likely voters are to know who they are. Getting voters' attention is only part of the problem, of course, but it is an essential part.

The second basic type of activity centers around the candidate's personal contact with potential voters. Most politicians have faith in the personal touch; if they can just talk to people and get them to listen, they can win their support. There is some evidence supporting this notion. Larry Pressler, now a senator from South Dakota, won his first House election in 1974 with a campaign that consisted largely of meeting people one-on-one. "I tried to shake 500 hard hands a day," Pressler has said. "That is where you really take their hand and look at them and talk to them a bit. I succeeding in doing that seven days a week. I put in a lot of twelve-hour days, starting at a quarter to six in the morning at some plant in Sioux Falls or Madison." [20] Pressler estimates that he shook 300–500 hands about 80 days. "You

[20] Alan L. Clem, "The Case of the Upstart Republican," in *The Making of Congressmen: Seven Campaigns of 1974*, ed. Alan L. Clem (North Scituate, Massachusetts: Duxbury Press, 1976), p. 140.

would not believe the physical and mental effort this requires." Shaking one hand per minute, a candidate would have to work for more than eight hours without stop to reach 500 people.[21]

The difficulty with this approach is that even House districts now contain about half a million people, and states can be much more populous. It is simply impossible to meet more than a small fraction of the electorate in the time frame of one or even several campaigns. But candidates often agree with Pressler that it is worth trying. Some go door-to-door, "shoeleathering" the neighborhoods. Many greet the early shift at the factory gate, shaking hands, passing out leaflets, showing workers that they care enough to get up as early as they do. Most will accept any opportunity to speak to a group and it is not uncommon for candidates to show up wherever people congregate in sufficient numbers: shopping centers, community picnics, parades, sporting events, and the like.

With the growing importance of television news, the candidate's activities have come to serve another purpose: getting the candidate free television exposure. Senate campaigns in particular have this aim. The main reason for walking the length of the state or working on an assembly line is that it makes news. Campaign events are designed not for the immediate audience so much as for the larger audience watching television at home. The temptation to resort to gimmickry is not always resisted. Bill Clark, running for a Democratic House nomination in Arkansas in 1976, passed out 20,000 candy bars as he made his campaign rounds; he did not get as many votes.[22]

The candidate's time is a scarce resource, so an important function of the campaign organization is to arrange that it be used effectively. An exhausting day of travel and meetings that results in few contacts with voters or little money raised is a campaign manager's nightmare. Time wasted cannot be retrieved. But candidates and their aides cannot tailor the social and political world to suit their needs; they have to be ready to exploit opportunities for meeting people as they arise. Again, experience and imagination are helpful.

[21] Ibid.
[22] "Outlook," C.Q. Weekly Report, p. 2990.

Campaign Messages

Along with letting voters know who the candidate is, the campaign is designed to persuade them to vote for him. Uncertainty dominates here as well. There is no magic formula for appealing to voters; what works in one district or election year may not work in another. The problem of appealing to voters is often rather different for incumbents, challengers, and candidates for open seats, so it is best to consider them separately.

Challengers certainly hope to convince people of their own virtues — at minimum, that they are qualified for the office[23] — but they are not likely to get far without directly undermining support for the incumbent. The trick is to find some vulnerable point to attack; there are a number of possibilities. Personal failings — moral lapses, felony convictions, signs of senility or alcoholism — offer obvious targets, although a surprising number of incumbents with such liabilities manage to win reelection.[24] Individual political failings — lack of attention to the district or to legislative duties, excessive junketing — also invite attack. One element in John LeBoutillier's defeat of incumbent Democrat Lester Wolff for New York's 6th District in 1980 was a series of radio commercials depicting Wolff as a habitual world traveler at the public's expense. "A seductive voice cooed the names of foreign cities Wolff had visited, while soft music, as in an airline lounge, was played." [25] But relatively few incumbents are open to serious public criticism on these grounds, and most challengers focus on more directly political behavior. They attack incumbents on the general ideological or partisan pattern of their votes, on specific votes, or on a combination of the two.

[23] Fenno, *Home Style,* p. 57.

[24] For example, Robert Leggett won reelection to the 4th District of California in 1976 even after having been a principal subject of the "Koreagate" investigation and having it known publicly that he had fathered two children by an aide, had been supporting two households for years, and had even forged his wife's name to the deed for the second house. For a more general analysis of the electoral effects of corruption charges, see John G. Peters and Susan Welch, "The Effects of Charges of Corruption on Voting Behavior in Congressional Elections," *American Political Science Review* 74 (1980):697–708.

[25] Roger H. Davidson and Walter J. Oleszek, *Congress and Its Members* (Washington, D.C.: Congressional Quarterly Press, 1981), p. 73.

Although cases are known where a single wrong vote cost a member of Congress his seat, it is by no means easy to nail a member with his voting record. Members are aware they may be called to answer for any vote and on controversial issues take pains to cast what Fenno calls an "explainable" vote.[26] That is, any vote that is likely to offend important groups in the member's electoral coalition or in the district at large will be cast only if it can be supported by a plausible explanation, one which does not make the member look bad, if it is questioned. Normally, a few "wrong" votes do not seriously weaken an incumbent; a string of them, however, lends plausibility to the charge that a member is mismatched with his constituency and ought to be replaced.

More general ideological or partisan attacks are commonly made but infrequently effective. Incumbents are criticized for being too liberal or too conservative for the constituency or for their guilt by association with unpopular parties or causes. This approach became less effective in the 1960s and 1970s as incumbents learned to avoid ideological categorization and responsibility for party decisions when it would hurt them politically back home. By soliciting support as individuals rather than as representatives of the party or cause, they undermine the force of such charges.

But not with perfect success. In 1980, for instance, Democratic Senators Frank Church of Idaho and Birch Bayh of Indiana were defeated by challengers who effectively attacked their liberal records as out of step with their states and the times. Dan Quayle, who defeated Bayh, also gleefully adopted the slogan Bayh had used eighteen years earlier to help him defeat a three-term incumbent: "18 years in Washington is long enough for one man."

Church and Bayh were among six Senate Democrats who were targeted for defeat by the National Conservative Political Action Committee (NCPAC), which mounted harshly negative campaigns against them more than a year before the election, long before it was known who their opponents would be. The campaigns, run independently of any candidate or party, aimed solely to discredit the incumbents, softening them up for who-

26 Fenno, *Home Style,* pp. 141–146.

ever turned out to be the challenger. The theme of the Idaho campaign was "ABC — Anybody but Church." Two other targeted Senate Democrats, John Culver of Iowa and George' McGovern of South Dakota, also lost, while the remaining two (Alan Cranston of California and Thomas Eagleton of Missouri) were reelected.

NCPAC claimed credit for defeating the incumbents, but all of them were in serious trouble with or without NCPAC, and even the challengers supposedly aided by the negative campaigns have criticized them as ineffective or even counterproductive, generating sympathy for their intended victims. This did not keep NCPAC from targeting more Democrats in the 1982 election; in 1981, more than twenty months before the election, NCPAC began running television spots attacking Paul Sarbanes, a liberal Democratic Senator from Maryland.[27] It is not yet clear whether other groups, perhaps with different ideological orientations, will imitate NCPAC; if they do, political life may become rather more unpleasant, if not riskier, for incumbents. Political dialogue will certainly become nastier.

Part of the national Republican effort in 1980 was designed to blame all Democratic congressional candidates for the federal government's failures. Apart from any particular campaign, television ads were run with the theme, "Vote Republican. For a Change." It is not certain what effect, if any, these ads had on voters, but they probably gave encouragement to Republican candidates and supporters.[28] Regardless of their immediate effect, these efforts raise the possibility of a reversal of the long-term trend away from collective toward individual responsibility among members of Congress. And if the trend were to go the other way, the consequences would be profound.

Incumbents have, up to now, also avoided the fallout from the public's overwhelmingly negative view of the Congress' institutional performance. Rather than defend the institution, they join in the criticism. "Members of Congress run *for* Congress by running *against* Congress." [29] They defend their own per-

---

[27] "Campaign '82," *C.Q. Weekly Report* 39 (October 31, 1981):2121.
[28] "Battle of Attrition for GOP Comeback Bid," *C.Q. Weekly Report* 38 (February 23, 1980):437.
[29] Fenno, *Home Style*, p. 168; emphasis is Fenno's.

formance vigorously but the collective actions of Congress not at all. Because of the way Congress operates, the blame for its failures is easily laid at the feet of others.[30]

It is obviously no easy matter to undermine an incumbent's support; the challenger's ability to do so depends largely on the incumbent's own behavior. In the search for campaign issues, challengers are necessarily opportunists. It is a matter of exploiting the incumbent's mistakes — neglect of the district, personal lapses, a string of "bad" votes — and if the incumbent avoids them, there is little the challenger can do.

Incumbents pursue reelection throughout their term in office, so their campaign strategies are visible in all their dealings with constituents. Naturally they try to avoid the mistakes that would give opponents campaign issues, but in an uncertain and complicated political world this is not always possible. So shrewd incumbents work to maintain the kind of relationship with constituents that will allow them to survive a damaging vote or a contrary political tide. Fenno's insightful account of how House members do this in fact describes effective campaigning by any congressional candidate, incumbent or otherwise.

Fenno traveled extensively with eighteen House members as they made the rounds of their districts. He found that each member projected a personal "home style" that defined his relationship to the groups he relied on for political support. Home styles varied according to the character of the district and the personality of the individual member. But in one way or another, all members basically sought to inspire *trust* among their constituents.[31] They did this by emphasizing their personal qualifications, including moral character, by identifying with their constituents ("I am one of you," they implied, "so you can trust me to make the right decisions — those you would make under the same circumstances"), and by working to develop bonds of empathy with the groups and individuals they met.

For most of them, issues, policy, and partisanship were *not* prominent objects of discussion with constituents and were not used to elicit support. Even members who did display an issue-oriented home style used issues primarily to cement ties of trust;

[30] Ibid., pp. 166–168.
[31] Ibid., p. 55.

how they addressed the issue rather than the issue itself is what mattered. Members used issues to show themselves to be the kind of people constituents would want in Washington.

Along with trust, members emphasized their *accessibility*. Constituents were reminded continually that the lines of communication were open, that they had access to the member whenever they needed it. The payoffs are clear. A member who is trusted and accessible, thought to be "one of us," will have much less trouble defending himself against political attack. His explanations for controversial votes will be heard more sympathetically; institutional or partisan failures, even notorious ethical lapses, may go unpunished.

This kind of relationship cannot be developed overnight, nor can it be maintained without continual reinforcement. Its importance is the reason why, as one congressman put it, "it's a personal franchise you hold, not a political franchise." [32] Seats are safe for individuals, not parties. Nonincumbents may aspire to it, but they have little chance to achieve it in the brief period of a single election campaign. Those who have held other elective offices in the district or who have run active campaigns previously have a head start.

Although incumbents, at least in the House, engage more or less continuously in activities aimed at assuring reelection, their real campaigns start when it becomes clear who the challenger will be: in the primary or general election or both. Different challengers present different problems and inspire different campaign strategies. Inept, obscure, or underfinanced opponents can be dealt with by routine maintainance of ties with groups in the electoral coalition and otherwise ignored. Ignoring the opposition is a standard tactic of incumbents who feel relatively secure; why give an unknown opponent free publicity?

More serious opponents compel more vigorous campaigns, with the strategy adapted to the relative strengths and weaknesses of both candidates. This kind of adjustment is evident in the thinking of a Democrat in Fenno's group:

> I pulled a lot of Republican votes last time that I'll lose this time — everywhere — and it will be worst in the few counties

[32] Quoted in ibid., p. 114.

I mentioned. My opponent has a strong identification with the Republican party, having been state chairman all those years. My last opponent never had that identification. He was a minister. . . . He was duck soup.[33]

Common to most incumbents' campaigns is an emphasis on the value of experience and seniority (for the capacity it gives members to serve the district more effectively) and reminders of the things the member has done over the years for his constituents. In special circumstances, special ploys may be necessary. Senator Milton Young, running for reelection to the Senate from North Dakota in 1974 at the age of seventy-six, countered suggestions that he was getting too old by running a TV spot showing him splitting a block of wood with a karate chop.[34]

Despite the knowledge members acquire of their constituencies, uncertainty plagues incumbents as well as nonincumbents. Each election may present a new challenge and a new set of electoral variables. Since incumbents are not sure which of the things they did got them elected previously, they cannot be sure what combination of campaign activities will serve them in altered circumstances. Although in any given election year, most incumbents are reelected easily (at least in the House), most of them have had close calls at one time or another and so feel much less secure than the simple reelection figures imply them to be.[35] All know of seemingly entrenched incumbents who suffered surprising defeats; Van Deerlin's fate will not be forgotten quickly.

Because of uncertainty, members tend to exaggerate electoral threats and to overreact to them. They are inspired by worst-case scenarios — what would they have to do to win if everything went wrong? — rather than probabilities.[36] Hence we find members who conduct full-scale campaigns even though the opposition is nowhere to be seen. Fenno's account of one member's

[33] Quoted in ibid., p. 15.

[34] Barone et al., *Almanac*, p. 669.

[35] John F. Bibby, Thomas E. Mann, and Norman J. Ornstein, *Vital Statistics on Congress, 1980* (Washington, D.C.: American Enterprise Institute for Public Policy Research, 1980), p. 17.

[36] Their campaign finance practices reflect this; see Jacobson, *Money*, pp. 121–122.

reaction to the pressures of uncertainty even under circumstances that should have added to his confidence is memorable:

> One October midnight, walking down a deserted city street, a member shouted into the empty darkness at his unseen opponent, whose campaign had been largely invisible, "Donald Fox! Why aren't you out campaigning? Donald Fox. Where the f_____ are you? [37]

The desire to win decisively enough to discourage future opposition also leads incumbents to campaign a good deal harder than would seem objectively necessary.

Candidates for open seats face somewhat different electoral situations because none of the contestants is an incumbent or challenger with the accompanying advantages or disadvantages. They are much more likely to have to win hard-fought primary contests to get the nomination, for the opportunity offered to ambitious politicians by an open seat attracts more and stronger candidates.[38] Indeed, the primary is often a more difficult hurdle than the general election.

Both candidates are likely to have some experience in elective office and so to have some familiarity with at least a part of the constituency and some useful relationships with electorally important segments of it. Both are likely to have adequate campaign resources because contests for open seats are notoriously competitive; the best chance to take a seat from the opposing party occurs when no incumbent is involved. As a consequence, candidates for open seats are typically better known and better liked than challengers — but not so well as incumbents.[39] No particular pattern of campaign strategy is typical of candidates for open seats other than a highly variable mixture of the approaches used by incumbents and challengers that coincides with their electoral position between the two.

Some typical characteristics of contests for open seats were evident in the race for California's 41st District in 1980. Incumbent Republican Bob Wilson's decision to retire after twenty-

[37] Quoted in Fenno, *Home Style*, p. 16.
[38] Harvey Schantz, "Contested and Uncontested Primaries for the U.S. House," *Legislative Studies Quarterly* 5 (1980):550; see also Table 3.4.
[39] The evidence is in the next chapter.

eight years in the House excited the ambition of a number of local politicians who had been waiting for just such an opportunity. Both parties had lively primary contests among candidates who were current or former officeholders. The Republican nomination went to Bill Lowery, a San Diego city councilman. The Democratic winner was another Bob Wilson, a state senator whose senate district coincided almost perfectly with the congressional district. He had entered politics as Robert Wilson, but changed his ballot name to "Bob" a few years later in what was interpreted as a ploy to profit from the confusion with the congressman.

The Lowery campaign took pains to see that he did not. It formed a committee of "Wilsons for Lowery," including the retiring congressman and San Diego mayor Pete Wilson. It also ran television spots of the Republican Wilson standing in front of the Capitol saying "This is Congressman Bob Wilson. *Don't vote for me!* Don't vote for Bob Wilson! Vote for Bill Lowery!" Lowery eventually won with 55 percent of the two-party vote; he spent $212,099 on his campaign; the losing Wilson spent even more, $395,946.[40]

Senate Campaigns

I observed in Chapter 3 that Senate elections are usually much more competitive than House elections; Senate incumbents do not win so easily or so frequently as do House incumbents. A number of mutually reinforcing explanations for this difference are implied by the discussion up to this point, and it is useful to bring them into sharper focus.

One reason Senate elections are more competitive is that Senate incumbents are usually faced with more formidable opponents. About two-thirds of the Senate challengers in the 1970s had previously held at least one elective office. Those who had not were often well known from other activities. Successful nonincumbent Senate candidates have in recent years included two former astronauts (John Glenn and Harrison Schmitt), a former

[40] Alan Ehrenhalt, ed., *Politics in America: Members of Congress in Washington and at Home* (Washington, D.C.: Congressional Quarterly Press, 1981), p. 176.

professional basketball star (Bill Bradley), a former presidential advisor and ambassador (Daniel Patrick Moynihan), and Elizabeth Taylor's sixth husband (John Warner).

Prominent challengers attract campaign resources. Senate campaigns in general attract proportionately greater contributions because the donations are, in a sense, more cost-effective. Senate elections are likely to be closer, so the collective impact of campaign resources is more likely to affect the outcome. Parties and groups with particular policy agendas are aware that, when it comes to passing legislation, one senator is worth 4.35 House members. The Republicans had to defeat far fewer incumbents to take over the Senate than they would have to to take over the House. It makes strategic sense for campaign contributors to focus on Senate seats, and that is what they have done. Thus Senate challengers are much more likely to enjoy adequate campaign financing.

Senate challengers can also use their campaign resources more effectively. Most Senate constituencies have the size and the structure to employ television efficiently. Resources are usually sufficient to justify using campaign professionals and the technical paraphernalia of modern campaigns: computers, polls, direct mail advertising and solicitation, and so forth. The news media are much more interested in Senate campaigns, so much more free attention and publicity is bestowed on Senate candidates than on their House counterparts. It is little wonder that Senate challengers and other nonincumbents are much better known by voters than are House challengers.[41]

Furthermore, Senate incumbents find it much more difficult to develop and maintain the kind of personal relationship with constituents that Fenno finds among House incumbents. The reason is obvious. Senate districts — states — are, with six exceptions, more populous than congressional districts, often very much so. The opportunities for personal contacts with constituents and attention to individual problems are proportionately fewer. Even the larger Senate staffs cannot make up the difference.

Senators' activities in Washington are also more conspicuous. Action in the Senate is more visible; the Senate has fewer mem-

[41] See Table 5.3.

bers, and they are given more attention by the news media. Senators are thus more likely to be associated with controversial and divisive issues. Usually they must try to represent constituencies that are much more socially and politically diverse than congressional districts. Senators do not have the pressure of a two-year election cycle to keep them attuned to the folks back home. Electoral coalitions may fall into disrepair, and a careless senator may discover that he must begin almost from scratch when reelection time rolls around.

The campaign finance laws also make it easier for national party organizations to intervene effectively in Senate contests; many of the Republican challengers who won in 1980 enjoyed substantial assistance from the national party committees. Senate challengers were helped early in the campaign, while Republican House challengers were generally ignored (see Table 6.12 in Chapter 6 for the evidence).

Not all incumbent senators are strongly challenged, of course, and when they are not, they win as easily as do most House incumbents.[42] Lopsided incumbent Senate victories are by no means rare. But they are much less the norm than in House contests.

[42] Mark C. Westlye, "Information and Partisanship in Senate Elections" (Paper delivered during the Annual Meeting of the American Political Science Association, New York, September 3–6, 1981).

5
Congressional Voters

Virtually every issue raised in the previous two chapters was examined from the perspective of some implicit notions about how congressional voters operate. Discussions of the sources of the incumbency advantage, the importance of campaign money, and House-Senate electoral differences, to mention a few examples, were all grounded in particular assumptions about voting behavior in congressional elections. So, too, are the campaign and career strategies of congressional candidates. Their activities are guided by beliefs about what sways voters, and at the same time they help to define the context in which voters must make their choices. An adequate understanding of voting behavior in congressional elections is important to congressional scholars and politicians alike. Neither group has reason to be fully satisfied; uncertainty afflicts scholars as well as candidates. But recent studies have produced a great deal of fresh information about congressional voters, and we know much more about them than we did just a few years back. This chapter, then, examines voting behavior in congressional elections and how it relates to the other phenomena of congressional election politics. It begins with a discussion of voter turnout, then turns to the fundamental question of how voters come to prefer one candidate to the other.

Turnout in Congressional Elections

Voting requires not only a choice among candidates, but also the decision to vote in the first place. A majority of Americans do not, in fact, vote in congressional elections. This has long been true of midterm elections and has now become the case in presidential election years as well. The information on turnout in elections for president and U.S. Representative is presented in Figure 5.1. Obviously, participation in congressional elections is strongly influenced by whether or not there is a presidential contest to attract voters to the polls; turnout drops by an average of 14 percentage points when there is not. Even in presidential election years, congressional voting is about 4 percentage points lower than presidential voting. After reaching a high point in the early 1960s, turnout at both the midterm and in presidential years has been declining steadily for twenty years.

These data raise a number of questions; not all of them have satisfactory answers. The most salient question — why the decline in turnout — has been the subject of intensive investigation but political scientists still lack a definitive answer. The mystery is all the deeper because the single demographic factor most strongly associated with participation — level of education — has been increasing in the population at the same time voting has been dropping.[1] The decrease in voting is surely linked in some way to the growing cynicism and distrust of political institutions mentioned in the introduction, but it is not clear exactly how. A full examination of the issue would take us too far afield; it is enough for our purposes to recognize that members of Congress are elected, collectively, by a shrinking proportion of eligible voters. In the most recent midterm election, 1978, little more than one-third of the adult population bothered to go to the polls.

The low level of voting in congressional elections raises a sec-

---

[1] Richard A. Brody, "The Puzzle of Political Participation in America," in *The New American Political System*, ed. Anthony King (Washington, D.C.: The American Enterprise Institute for Public Policy Research, 1978), pp. 296–297.

FIGURE 5.1
Turnout in Presidential and House Elections, 1932–1980

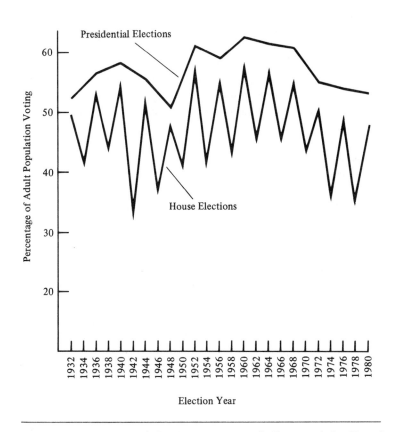

Source: U.S. Bureau of the Census, *Statistical Abstract of the United States,* 101st edition. (Washington, D.C.: Government Printing Office, 1980), Table 851.

ond question: Who votes and who does not? The question is important because politicians wanting to get into Congress or to remain there will be most responsive to the concerns of people they expect will vote. If voters and nonvoters have noticeably different needs or preferences, the former are likely to be served, the latter slighted.

The question of who votes and who does not has been studied most thoroughly by Raymond Wolfinger and Steven Rosenstone. They find that turnout is affected most strongly by education; the more years of formal education, the more likely one is to vote. Voting also increases with income and occupational status, but these are themselves strongly related to education and have only a modest influence on turnout once it is taken into account.[2] Voting also increases with age, and some occupational groups — notably farmers and government workers — show distinctly higher levels of participation than their other demographic characteristics would lead us to expect. Other things equal, turnout is also about 6 percentage points lower among people living in the south.[3]

Wolfinger's and Rosenstone's demonstration that turnout varies most strongly with education comes as no surprise, since every other study of American voting behavior has found this to be the case. The accepted explanation is that education imparts knowledge about politics and increases one's capacity to deal with complex and abstract matters like those found in the political world.[4] People with the requisite cognitive skills and political knowledge find the cost of processing and acting on political information lower and the satisfactions greater. Politics is less threatening and more interesting. In a similar manner, learning outside of formal education can facilitate participation. People whose occupations put them in close touch with politics and governmental policy — government workers and farmers — vote more consistently, as do people who simply have longer experience as adults.

Curiously, the connection between education and voting participation does *not* hold in most other Western-style democracies. Western Europeans of lower education and occupational status vote at least as consistently as the rest of the population. The reason, according to Walter Dean Burnham, is that the strong European parties of the left provide the necessary political information and stimuli to their chosen clientele. The

---

[2] Raymond E. Wolfinger and Steven J. Rosenstone, *Who Votes?* (New Haven: Yale University Press, 1980), pp. 24–26.

[3] Ibid., p. 94.

[4] Ibid., p. 18.

sharply lower turnout at the lower end of the American socio-economic scale can thus be interpreted as another consequence of weak parties interested only in electoral politics and patronage.[5]

Better educated, wealthier, higher-status, older people are, for whatever reason, clearly overrepresented in the electorate. If their preferences and concerns were substantially different from those of nonvoters, governmental policy might well be biased in their favor. Wolfinger and Rosenstone, citing recent survey data, argue that the views of voters are not very different from those of the population as a whole, so differential participation does not impart any special bias.[6] Current policy positions do not divide people along socioeconomic lines. But if policy issues arise that do divide people according to wealth or age or status, representation of preferences will be skewed. The treatment of the Reagan administration's economic policies in the 97th Congress offers something of a test of this notion. The powerful and successful resistance to reductions in social security benefits obviously reflects the respect politicians have for the electoral clout of older voters. The weak and futile defense of social welfare programs is probably a consequence of the knowledge that so many of these programs' beneficiaries do not vote.

Another question posed by the turnout data is whether congressional electorates differ between presidential and midterm election years. Do the millions of citizens who only vote for congressional candidates because they happen to be on the same ballot with presidential candidates change the electoral environment in politically consequential ways? One prominent study, based on surveys of voters taken in the 1950s, concluded that they did. The electorate in presidential years was found to be composed of a larger proportion of voters weakly attached to either political party and more subject to political phenomena peculiar to the specific election, notably their feelings about the presidential candidates. At the midterm, with such voters making up a much smaller proportion of the electorate, partisanship

[5] Walter Dean Burnham, "Shifting Patterns of Congressional Voting Participation in the United States" (Paper delivered during the Annual Meeting of the American Political Science Association, New York, September 3–6, 1981).

[6] Wolfinger and Rosenstone, *Who Votes?*, pp. 104–114.

prevailed. The consequence was a pattern of "surge and decline," in which the winning presidential candidate's party picked up congressional seats (the surge), many of which were subsequently lost at the next midterm election when the pull of the presidential candidate was no longer operating (the decline). This explained why, in every midterm election since 1934, the president's party lost seats in the House.[7]

Aggregate shifts in congressional seats and votes from one election to the next will be examined at length in the next chapter. At this point, suffice it to say that the view of electorates underlying this theory has not been supported by subsequent evidence. More recent research suggests that midterm voters are no more or less partisan than those in presidential years and share the same distribution of demographic characteristics.[8] The addition or subtraction of voters drawn out by a presidential contest does not seem to produce significantly different electorates. This does not mean that presidential elections might not affect congressional elections in other ways, to be sure; that issue is taken up later.

These observations about turnout refer to the electorate as a whole, but congressional candidates are of course much more concerned about the particular electorates in their states and districts. As noted in Chapter 2, turnout is by no means the same across constituencies; it varies enormously. One obvious source of variation is the demographic makeup of the district: average level of education, income, occupational status, and so on. These factors are, at least in the short run, fairly constant in any individual state or district; but turnout also varies in the same constituency from election to election (quite apart from the presidential year-midterm difference), and these variations are, for our purposes, the most interesting.

The generally low level of voting in congressional elections means that a large measure of the fundamental electoral cur-

---

[7] Angus Campbell, "Surge and Decline: A Study of Electoral Change," in *Elections and the Political Order*, Angus Campbell et al. (New York: John Wiley, 1966), pp. 40–62.

[8] Except that midterm electorates are somewhat older. See Raymond E. Wolfinger, Steven J. Rosenstone, and Richard A. McIntosh, "Presidential and Congressional Voters Compared," *American Politics Quarterly* 9 (1981):245–255.

rency — votes — lies untapped. This affects campaign strategy in several ways. Even incumbents who have been winning by healthy margins recognize that many citizens did not vote *for* them (even if they did not vote against them) and that they could be in trouble if an opponent comes along who can mobilize the abstainers. This is not an idle worry. Generally, the higher the turnout, the closer the election; the lower the turnout, the more easily the incumbent is reelected.[9] Successful challengers evidently draw to the polls many people who normally do not bother to vote. The wisdom of defusing the opposition and discouraging strong challenges is again apparent. Experienced campaigners know that getting one's supporters to the polls is as important as winning their support in the first place; well-organized campaigns typically devote a major share of their work to getting out the vote.

The effort to get out the vote presupposes that there is a vote to be gotten out, that people brought to the polls will indeed support the candidate. For what finally matters is what voters do in the voting booth. And this raises a question of fundamental interest to politicians and political scientists alike. What determines how people vote for congressional candidates? What moves voters to support one candidate rather than the other? The entire structure of congressional election politics hinges on the way voters reach this decision.

Partisanship in Congressional Elections

Partisanship was, until fairly recently, understood to be the strongest influence on congressional voters. And even though the effects of party ties have weakened over the past two decades, party is still a major influence on the vote choice. The pioneering survey studies of voting behavior in both presidential and congressional elections conducted in the 1950s found that a large majority of voters thought of themselves as Democrats or Republicans and voted accordingly. Particular candidates or issues might, on occasion, persuade a person to vote for someone of the

[9] Turnout is positively related to the challenger's share of the vote even when party strength and campaign expenditures are controlled.

other party, but the defection was likely to be temporary and did not dissolve the partisan attachment.[10]

The leading interpretation of these findings was that voters who were willing to label themselves Democrats or Republicans identified with the party in the same way they might identify with a region or ethnic or religious group: "I'm a Texan, a Baptist, and a Democrat." The psychological attachment to a party was rooted in powerful personal experiences (best exemplified by the millions who became Democrats during the New Deal), or was learned, along with similar attachments, from the family. In either case, identification with a party was thought to establish an enduring orientation toward the political world. The result, in aggregate, was a stable pattern of partisanship across the entire electorate. Thus from the New Deal onward, the Democrats enjoyed consistent national majorities. Individual states or congressional districts were, in many cases, "safe" for candidates of one party or the other.

This did not mean that the same party won every election, of course. Some voters did not think of themselves as belonging to a party, and even those who did would defect if their reactions to particular candidates or issues or recent events ran contrary to their party identification strongly enough. But once these short-term forces were no longer present, the long-term influence of party identification would reassert itself and they would return to their partisan moorings. Only quite powerful and unusual experiences could inspire permanent shifts of party allegiance for most citizens.

This interpretation of party identification has been threatened from at least two directions since it was developed. First, the electoral influence of partisanship has diminished steadily over the last twenty years. Fewer voters are willing to consider themselves partisans, and the party attachments of those who do are likely to be weaker. The percentage of people declaring themselves to be strong partisans fell from 36 percent in 1952 to 26 percent in 1980. Even those who still admit to partisan attachments are a good deal more likely to defect to candidates of the

---

[10] See Angus Campbell, Philip E. Converse, Warren E. Miller, and Donald E. Stokes, *The American Voter* (New York: John Wiley, 1960), ch. 6.

other party than they once were.[11] Party loyalty among voters is plainly not what it used to be. The steady weakening of partisan ties is abundantly evident in congressional elections, as will be apparent shortly.

Although no definitive explanation for the decline of electoral partisanship has been developed, it is no doubt related to political events of the past two decades. Each party brought disaster upon itself by nominating a presidential candidate preferred only by its more extreme ideologues: the Republicans with Goldwater in 1964, the Democrats with McGovern in 1972. In 1968, the Vietnam War and the civil rights issue split the Democrats badly and fostered the strongest third-party showing since 1924. Republicans suffered in turn as the Watergate revelations forced their disgraced president from office. Jimmy Carter's inept handling of the economy and troubles with Iran laid the Democrats low in 1980. More generally, the political alliances formed in the battles over the New Deal were fractured along multiple lines as new problems and issues forced their way onto the political agenda.

Voters responded to these political phenomena as they were expected to respond to short-term forces, defecting when their party preferences were contradicted strongly enough. But as defections became more widespread and partisanship in general continued to decline, an interpretation of party identification which, among other things, more easily accommodated change, became more persuasive. The alternative interpretation emphasizes the practical rather than psychological aspects of party identification. It has been presented most thoroughly by Morris P. Fiorina, who argues that people attach themselves to a party because they have found, through past experience, that candidates of the party are more likely than those of the other to produce the kinds of results they prefer. Since it is costly of time and energy to find out the full range of information on all of the candidates who run for the many offices filled by election in the United States, voters quite reasonably use the shorthand cue of party to simplify the voting decision. Past experience is a more

[11] Warren E. Miller, Arthur H. Miller, and Edward J. Schneider, *American National Election Studies Data Sourcebook 1952–1978* (Cambridge: Harvard University Press, 1980), pp. 334, 376, 383–384.

useful criterion than future promises or expectations because it is more certain. Party cues are recognized as imperfect, to be sure, and people who are persuaded that a candidate of the other party would deal more effectively with their concerns vote for him or her. More importantly, if cumulative experience suggests that candidates of the preferred party are no longer predictably superior in this respect, the party preference naturally decays.[12] Party ties are subject to modification by the answer to the question, "What have you done for me *lately*?" [13] The virtue of this approach is that it can account for both the observed short-run stability and long-run lability of party identification evident in individuals and the electorate.

The literature on party identification is large, and the concept is currently undergoing the most thorough reinvestigation since its original presentation.[14] The issue of which interpretation is preferable (or which combination — they are by no means irreconcilable) will not be settled here. What matters most for our purposes is that however party identification is interpreted, it remains an important influence on congressional voters, but that this influence has diminished and is now a good deal weaker than it once was. Congressional voters are therefore more readily swayed by other phenomena of electoral politics, most importantly the individual candidates.

The declining influence of party identification in congressional elections is evident from the figures in Table 5.1. It is clearly not a consequence of increased political independence; the share of the electorate composed of independent voters who lean toward neither party has not grown. What has grown is the proportion of voters who vote contrary to their expressed party affiliation. Defections in House elections are more than twice as common now as they were in the 1950s. Senate electorates have reached, by a somewhat more erratic path, a similar state, with about 20 percent of the voters commonly defecting.

---

[12] Morris P. Fiorina, *Retrospective Voting in American National Elections* (New Haven: Yale University Press, 1981).

[13] Samuel L. Popkin, John W. Gorman, Charles Phillips, and Jeffrey A. Smith, "Comment: What Have You Done for Me Lately? Toward an Investment Theory of Voting," *American Political Science Review* 70 (1976): 779–805.

[14] See the NES/CPS American National Election Study, 1980.

TABLE 5.1
Party-Line Voters, Defectors, and Independents in House and Senate
Elections, 1956–1980 (in percentages)

	House Elections			Senate Elections		
Year	Party-line Voters	Defectors	Pure Independents	Party-line Voters	Defectors	Pure Independents
1956	82	9	9	79	12	9
1958	84	11	5	85	9	5
1960	80	12	8	77	15	8
1962	83	12	6	—*	—	—
1964	79	15	5	78	16	6
1966	76	16	8	—	—	—
1968	74	19	7	74	19	7
1970	76	16	8	78	12	10
1972	75	17	8	69	22	9
1974	74	18	8	73	19	8
1976	72	19	9	70	19	11
1978	69	22	9	71	20	9
1980	69	23	8	71	21	8

* Data not available.

Sources: House Elections: Thomas E. Mann and Raymond E. Wolfinger, "Candidates and Parties in Congressional Elections," *American Political Science Review* (September, 1980). Reprinted by permission; NES/CPS 1980 National Election Study; *Senate elections:* tabulated from SRC/CPS National Election Studies, 1956–1980, by Eric Smith of the University of California State Date Program, Berkeley, California.

The decline of party loyalty has had profound consequences for House elections because the growth in defections has been entirely at the expense of challengers. This is evident from the data in Table 5.2. The years selected are typical of their period. Voters sharing the incumbent's party are as loyal now as they ever were. Voters of the challenger's party have become much less faithful and at present are as likely as not to vote for the (incumbent) candidate of the other party. Defections now also favor Senate incumbents, but by a much narrower margin.

These figures display, at the level of individual voters, the augmented advantage of House incumbents that was evident in

TABLE 5.2
Partisan Voters Defecting to Incumbents and Challengers (in percentages)

Year	Defecting to Incumbents	Defecting to Challengers
House Elections		
1958	16	9
1960	19	9
1968	33	14
1970	32	5
1978	54	5
1980	48	9
Senate Elections		
1978	33	11
1980	32	15

Source: SRC/CPS National Election Studies.

the aggregate figures discussed in Chapter 3. They also reiterate the familiar House-Senate differences in this regard. But they do not explain either phenomenon. As Albert Cover has pointed out, there is no logical reason why weaker party ties could not produce defections balanced between incumbents and challengers or even favoring the latter.[15] After all, voters are about as likely to desert their party in Senate as in House elections, but the defections are not nearly as likely to favor incumbents. Other factors must be involved.

Information and Voting

One factor involved is *information*. At the most basic level, people hesitate to vote for candidates they know nothing at all about. Among the most consistent findings produced by studies of congressional voters over the past generation is that simple knowledge of who the candidates are has a striking impact on voting behavior. Prior to the 1978 election study, knowledge of

[15] Albert D. Cover, "One Good Term Deserves Another: The Advantage of Incumbency in Congressional Elections," *American Journal of Political Science* 21 (1977):532.

the candidates was measured by whether or not voters remembered their names when asked by an interviewer. Very few partisans defect if they remember the name of their own party's candidate but not that of the opponent; more than half usually defect if they remember only the name of the other party's candidate; defection rates of voters who know both or neither fall in between. The pattern holds for Senate as well as House elections.[16]

This suggested an important reason why incumbents do so well in House elections: voters are much more likely to remember their names. Typically, 50 to 60 percent can recall the incumbent's name, 20 to 30 percent that of the challenger. If only one of the two candidates is remembered, it is the incumbent 95 percent of the time. But understanding the effects of differential knowledge of the candidates' names does not clear up all the basic questions.

It does not, first of all, explain the growth in partisan defection to incumbents. Beyond question, incumbents are relatively much better known because they enjoy abundant resources for advertising themselves in a variety of ways and exploit them vigorously. But as these resources grew (along with their electoral margins), their advantage in familiarity among voters did not.[17] House incumbents are remembered no more frequently, and their advantage in this regard over challengers is no greater in 1980 than it was in 1958. Second, voters favor incumbents even when they cannot recall either candidate's name, so there must be more to the choice than simple name familiarity.[18] Voters are, in fact, often willing to offer opinions about candidates — incumbents and challengers alike — even when they cannot remember their names.[19]

[16] Gary C. Jacobson, *Money in Congressional Elections* (New Haven: Yale University Press, 1980), p. 16.

[17] John A. Ferejohn, "On the Decline of Competition in Congressional Elections," *American Political Science Review* 71 (1977):170.

[18] Ibid., p. 171; also Candice J. Nelson, "The Effects of Incumbency on Voting in Congressional Elections, 1964–1974" (Paper delivered during the Annual Meeting of the American Political Science Association, Chicago, September 2–5, 1976), pp. 11–14.

[19] Jacobson, *Money*, pp. 19–20; also Alan I. Abramowitz, "Name Familiarity, Reputation, and the Incumbency Effect in a Congressional Election," *Western Political Quarterly* 28 (1975):668–684.

Such discoveries forced scholars to reconsider what is meant by "knowing" the candidates. Thomas Mann was first to show that many voters who could not recall a candidate's name could *recognize* the name from a list, information always available in the voting booth.[20] The two most recent national survey studies of congressional elections (1978 and 1980) have thus included questions testing both the voter's ability to recall and to recognize each candidate's name. They also include a battery of questions designed to find out what else voters know about the candidates, what sorts of contact they have had with them, and what they think of them on a variety of dimensions. The new data they produced allow a much more thorough examination of voting behavior in congressional elections than has been possible previously; they are the center of attention in the rest of this chapter. But unfortunately they cannot cast much light on what *changes* have occurred in patterns of congressional voting, since comparable data from earlier elections do not exist.[21]

The most recent studies of congressional voters leave no doubt, first of all, that voters recognize candidates' names much more readily than they recall them.[22] Table 5.3 presents the relevant data. House voters are more than twice as likely to recognize as to recall candidates in any incumbency category. The same is true of Senate voters, except in the case of incumbents, whose names are already recalled by more than half the voters.

These figures also leave no doubt that the House incumbents' advantage in recall is matched by an advantage in recognition. Nearly every voter recognizes the incumbent's name. The shift in focus from name recall to name recognition nicely resolves the apparent anomaly of voters favoring incumbents without know-

[20] Thomas E. Mann, *Unsafe at Any Margin: Interpreting Congressional Elections* (Washington, D.C.: American Enterprise Institute for Public Policy Research, 1978), pp: 30–34.

[21] For consideration of the difficulties of making comparisons over time using available data, see Morris P. Fiorina, "Congressmen and their Constituents: 1958 and 1978," in *Proceedings of the Thomas P. O'Neill, Jr. Symposium on the U.S. Congress,* ed. Dennis Hale (Chestnut Hill, Massachusetts: Boston College, forthcoming).

[22] The "feeling thermometer" was used to test whether the respondent recognized a candidate's name. Respondents were asked to indicate their degree of warmth or coldness toward a list of individuals on a scale of 0 to 100. If they did not recognize a name listed, they were to say so and proceed to the next without offering a "temperature."

TABLE 5.3
Incumbency Status and Voter Familiarity with Congressional Candidates, 1980 (in percentages)

Elections	Recalled Name	Recognized Name*	Neither
House			
Incumbents	46	92	8
Challengers	21	54	46
Open seats	32	82	19
Senate			
Incumbents	61	99	1
Challengers	40	81	19
Open seats	47	89	11

* Includes only respondents who reported voting and who could recognize and rate the candidate on the feeling thermometer or, if they could not rate the candidate, could recall the candidate's name.

Source: NES/CPS American National Election Study, 1980.

ing who they are. Many more voters also recognize the challenger than recall his name, but they still amount to only about half the sample. Candidates for open seats are better known than challengers but not so well known as incumbents; indeed, the data will show that they fall between incumbents and challengers on almost every measure. This is exactly what we would expect knowing the kinds of candidates and campaigns typical of open-seat contests.

Senate candidates are better known than their House counterparts in each category, and Senate incumbents are clearly better known than their challengers. But the gap is not nearly so wide as it is for House candidates. Again, this is the kind of pattern we would anticipate in light of the distinctive circumstances of Senate electoral politics outlined in the previous chapter.

Familiarity is considered important, of course, because of its connection to the vote. This is shown for the 1980 House and Senate elections in Table 5.4. In both kinds of elections, the more familiar voters are with a candidate, the more likely they

TABLE 5.4
Familiarity with Candidates and Voting Behavior in the 1980
Congressional Elections (percentage of voters defecting)

	Familiarity with Own Party's Candidate			
Elections	Recalled Name	Recognized Name	Neither	Marginal Total
House				
Familiarity with other party's candidate:				
Recalled name	28	67	80	46
Recognized name*	8	27	62	32
Neither	2	0	19	5
Marginal Total	18	21	55	28
Senate				
Familiarity with other party's candidate:				
Recalled name	22	46	80	27
Recognized name[a]	9	26	69	25
Neither	7	4	6	6
Marginal Total	18	26	44	23

* Recognized name and could rate the candidate on the thermometer scale.
Source: NES/CPS American National Election Study, 1980.

are to vote for him, with the effect also depending, in the same way, on the degree of familiarity with the other candidate. Defections are concentrated in the upper right-hand corner of each table; party loyalty predominates in the lower left-hand corner. Only 2 percent of the House voters and 7 percent of the Senate voters defect to candidates who are less familiar than their own; 70 percent of the former and 59 percent of the latter defect to candidates who are more familiar. Similarly, independents vote for the better-known candidate more than 80 percent of the time.

Why is familiarity of so much benefit to congressional candi-

TABLE 5.5

Familiarity, Incumbency Status, and Voters' Likes and Dislikes of House Candidates in 1980

	Recalled Name	Recognized Name[*]	Neither	Marginal Total
Percentage *liking* something about:				
Incumbents	75	50	13	58
Challengers	36	21	2	15
Candidates for open seats	55	40	0	36
Percentage *disliking* something about:				
Incumbents	32	13	8	21
Challengers	31	11	3	11
Candidates for open seats	42	19	0	23

[*] Recognized name and could rate the candidate on the thermometer scale but could not recall candidate's name.

Source: NES/CPS American National Election Study, 1980.

dates? The answer proposed by Donald Stokes and Warren Miller, that "in the main, to be perceived at all is to be perceived favorably," [23] has not found much support in later work.[24] It does not work that simply. Survey respondents were asked in 1980 what they liked and disliked about House candidates. As the figures in Table 5.5 indicate, the more familiar voters are with candidates, the more likely they are to find things they *both* like and dislike about them. Familiarity by no means breeds only favorable responses. More importantly, the benefits of incumbency obviously extend far beyond greater familiarity. Incumbents are better liked — by a wide margin — as well as better known than are challengers. At any level of familiarity, voters are more inclined to mention something they like about the in-

[23] Donald E. Stokes and Warren E. Miller, "Party Government and the Saliency of Congress," *Elections and the Political Order,* p. 205.

[24] Abramowitz, "Name Familiarity," pp. 673–683; Jacobson, *Money,* p. 16.

TABLE 5.6
Voters' Ratings of House and Senate Candidates on the 100-Point
Thermometer Scale, 1980, by Incumbency Status (averages)

Status	House Candidates		Senate Candidates	
Incumbents	65.9	(91.8) *	57.9	(98.4)
Challengers	52.3	(52.7)	53.3	(80.5)
Candidates for open seats	58.1	(79.8)	56.6	(89.1)

* Percentage of voters able to rate candidate.
Source: NES/CPS American National Election Study, 1980.

cumbent than about the challenger; negative responses are rather evenly divided, so the net benefit is clearly to the incumbent.

Voters were not asked what they liked or disliked about Senate candidates, but another evaluative dimension can be used to compare voters' feelings about House and Senate candidates. The survey asked respondents who could recognize a candidate to rate him on a scale of 0 to 100, with 0 the most unfavorable, 100 the most favorable, and 50 as neutral. The mean "thermometer" ratings, as they are called, for 1980 House and Senate candidates in different incumbency categories are shown in Table 5.6. House and Senate challengers are rated about the same (the important difference lying in the proportion of voters who could rate them at all; see Table 5.4), as are candidates for open seats. But House incumbents are substantially better regarded than Senate incumbents and so have a much larger advantage over challengers.[25]

Contacting Voters

Why are House incumbents so much better known and liked than their opponents? Why are Senate challengers more familiar to voters than House challengers? One obvious explana-

[25] A similar pattern was evident in 1978, although Senate challengers were regarded somewhat more favorably that year. See Barbara Hinckley, "House Re-elections and Senate Defeats: The Role of the Challenger," British Journal of Political Science 10 (1980):453.

tion is that messages about them reach voters more frequently. The percentage of voters reporting various sorts of contact with House and Senate candidates in 1978 [26] are reported in Table 5.7. Voters are more than twice as likely to report contact of every kind with incumbents than with challengers in House races. Almost every voter was reached in some way by the incumbent, while a majority of voters had no contact at all with the challenger. Senate incumbents, in contrast, have only a small advantage over challengers in frequency of reported contacts.

The differences between House and Senate challengers are sharpest in the area of mass media publicity. Notice especially the difference in the proportion of voters reached through television. Richard Fenno's observations of Senators and Senate candidates have led him to conclude that a major difference between House and Senate elections is the much greater importance of the mass media in the latter. The news media are much more interested in Senate candidates because they are much more interested in Senators.[27] As noted in the previous chapter, Senate campaigns are also wealthier and can use paid television more extensively and more efficiently than can House campaigns. The consequences are evident in the survey data; both factors enhance the Senate challenger's ability to catch the attention of voters, an essential ingredient of electoral success.

The table also supports Fenno's explanation of why Senate incumbents are less popular and more vulnerable than House incumbents quite apart from the different kinds of challengers they attract. Voters are twice as likely to have had some kind of face-to-face interaction with the House incumbent or his staff. Twenty-three percent of the voters claim to have met the House incumbent personally; only 9 percent say the same about the Senate incumbent. The feelings of trust that bind constituents to House members are nurtured by personal contacts and the promise of access. All but a few senators have no chance to forge such ties because their constituencies are simply too large. They are more remote, reaching voters almost entirely through the mass media. And often they do not control the message; the

[26] The contact questions were not asked about Senate candidates in 1980.
[27] Richard F. Fenno, Jr., *The United States Senate: A Bicameral Perspective* (Washington, D.C.: American Enterprise Institute, forthcoming), p. 11.

TABLE 5.7

Voters' Contacts with Congressional Candidates in 1978 (in percentages)

Type of Contact	House			Senate		
	Incumbent	Challenger	Open Seat	Incumbent	Challenger	Open Seat
Any	90	44	73	94	82	88
Met personally	23	4	14	9	5	9
Saw at meeting	20	3	13	10	5	13
Talked to staff	12	2	13	6	4	9
Received mail	71	16	43	53	32	47
Read about in newspaper or magazine	71	32	57	73	63	78
Heard on radio	34	15	28	45	37	49
Saw on TV	50	24	48	80	70	78
Family or friend had contact	39	11	26	—	—	—
Number =	(756)	(756)	(121)	(409)	(409)	(158)

Source: Thomas E. Mann and Raymond E. Wolfinger, "Candidates and Parties in Congressional Elections," *American Political Science Review* 74 (September, 1980). Reprinted by permission. Data are from the NES/CPS American National Election Study, 1978.

news media's greater interest in them is a mixed blessing. Senators are accorded more attention but are also subject to higher expectations. A House member running for the Senate explained it to Fenno this way:

> People don't treat me differently. They don't see any difference between the two jobs. Maybe they think it's a higher office, but that doesn't make any difference. But the media hold me to a much higher standard than they did as a House member. They expect me to know more details. Am I treated differently running for the Senate? By the people, no; by the media. yes.[28]

House incumbents normally do not attract much attention from the news media. This means that, except during campaigns, they produce and disseminate much of the information about themselves that reaches the public. To a large extent, they control their own press; no wonder it is a good press, and no wonder voters tend to think highly of them.[29] In most cases, only a vigorous campaign by the challenger spreads information critical of their performance, with effects that are analyzed later in this chapter.

Table 5.8 also reinforces the vital point that all nonincumbent House candidates are not alike. Voters report more contacts of all sorts with candidates for open seats than with challengers. The former generate figures which are often closer to those for incumbents than to those for challengers. (The major exception is significant: contacts through the mails, clear evidence of the value of the frank.) House incumbents do not hold such a wide advantage over challengers on these dimensions simply because they are incumbents and their opponents are not. Their opponents are, rather, much weaker candidates than they might be — or than appear when no incumbent is running. This is a natural consequence of the strategies followed by potential House candidates and their potential supporters discussed in Chapter 3.

The relationship between various kinds of contact, combined

[28] Ibid., pp. 18–19.
[29] Alan I. Abramowitz, "A Comparison of Voting for U.S. Senator and Representative in 1978," *American Political Science Review* 74 (1980): 639.

into four basic modes,[30] and voters' knowledge and evaluations of candidates, is shown in Table 5.8. Voters who report any kind of contact are more familiar with the candidate and are more likely to offer evaluative comments. Personal contact generally makes the most difference, particularly with regard to favorable comments, but some self-selection is doubtlessly involved; this kind of contact requires some effort on the part of respondents, more likely if the respondent knows and likes the candidate in the first place. Indirect "word-of-mouth" contact through experiences of family and friends is also effective (confirming politicians' faith in the ripple effects of their work to reach voters). Contact via the mails — letters and literature sent directly to individuals at home — appears to be a bit more effective than contact through the mass media.

Contacts are related to how well voters know and like candidates and all these factors are linked in some way to incumbency. A clearer depiction of how these variables are connected is provided by multiple regression analysis. A description of the variables used in the regression equations that follow in this chapter can be found in Table 5.9. Multiple regression allows us to measure the impact of several independent variables on a dependent variable, controlling for the effects of the other independent variables. Table 5.10 lists a set of regression equations measuring the relative impact of the four types of contact, plus two additional independent variables — the respondent's degree of interest in the election and the amount of money the candidate spent on the campaign — on the respondent's degree of familiarity with the candidate (the dependent variable in this equation).

First compare the intercepts, which estimate the value of the dependent variable when the values of all of the independent variables are set at zero. Notice that voters are quite familiar with incumbents even in the absence of contacts, interest in the

[30] Personal contact is defined as having met the candidate, attended a meeting where he spoke, or having contact with the candidate's staff; mail contact is receiving something in the mail from the candidate; mass media contact is learning about the candidate by reading newspapers and magazines, listening to the radio, or watching television; family and friends contact is reporting that a family member or acquaintance has had some kind of contact with the candidate.

Contacts, Familiarity, and Voters' Likes and Dislikes of House Candidates in 1978 (in percentages)

Type of Contact	Familiarity			Likes and Dislikes		Number of Cases
	Recall Name	Recognize Name	Neither	Like Something	Dislike Something	
Incumbents						
None	21	73	27	23	10	63
Any	53	96	4	68	19	676
Personal	67	100	0	85	27	260
Mail	58	98	2	71	21	538
Mass media	54	96	4	70	20	605
Family and friends	64	100	0	81	25	300
Challengers						
None	4	24	76	2	3	415
Any	32	74	26	23	25	334
Personal	48	92	8	50	48	48
Mail	43	80	20	34	30	125
Mass media	35	76	24	43	26	305
Family and friends	48	82	18	35	37	83
Candidates for open seats						
None	13	43	57	13	3	60
Any	49	88	12	44	22	176
Personal	52	96	4	71	29	52
Mail	51	90	10	52	26	102
Mass media	50	89	11	45	22	161
Family and friends	71	98	2	59	33	61

Source: NES/CPS American National Election Study, 1978.

TABLE 5.9
Definitions of Regression Equation Variables[*]

Respondent's vote	1 if Democratic, 0 if Republican
Party identification	1 if strong, weak, or independent Democrat, 0 if independent-independent, −1 if strong, weak, or independent Republican
Democrat is incumbent	1 if Democrat is incumbent, 0 otherwise
Republican is incumbent	1 if Republican is incumbent, 0 otherwise
Familiarity with Democrat Familiarity with Republican	1 if respondent recalls candidate's name, .5 if name is recognized but not recalled, 0 if name is not recognized or recalled
Likes something about Democrat Dislikes something about Democrat Likes something about Republican Dislikes something about Republican	For each variable, 1 if respondent mentions anything liked (or disliked) about the candidate, 0 otherwise
Democrat's thermometer rating Republican's thermometer rating	Respondent's feeling towards candidates on a scale of 0 to 100; respondents who do not know or rate candidate are placed at 50
Contact with Democrat Contact with Republican	1 if respondent reports having had any contact with candidate, 0 if not
Type of contact: Personal	1 if respondent has met candidate, attended a meeting where candidate spoke, or had contact with staff, 0 otherwise
Mail	1 if respondent received anything in the mail about the candidate, 0 if not
Mass media	1 if respondent learned about candidate by reading newspapers and magazines, listening to the radio, or watching television, 0 otherwise

[*] Used in Tables 5.10–5.13, 5.18, 6.4

TABLE 5.9 (continued)

Family and friends	1 if respondent's family or friends had any contact with the candidate, 0 if not
Campaign expenditures	Candidate's campaign expenditures in $100,000's
Interest in the campaign	1 if respondent was very much interested in the campaigns, 0 if not

election, or campaign expenditures. They typically reach .47 on the familiarity scale even when the values of the other variables are 0. Under the same conditions, challengers are, typically, almost completely unknown (at .08 on a scale, which runs from 0 to 1.0). Candidates for open seats fall in between incumbents and challengers on this measure.

The equations show that nonincumbent candidates benefit most from mass media contacts. The regression coefficients, which estimate how much change in the dependent variable is brought about by changes of one unit in the independent variables, are .28 and .30 on this variable, respectively, for challengers and candidates for open seats. That is, nonincumbents are that much more familiar to voters (on the scale of 0 to 1.0) whom they have reached through the mass media. These coefficients are much more than twice as large as their standard errors and therefore far exceed this customary minimum required for statistical significance. Other forms of contact generally add something to familiarity beyond that gained through mass media contact, but they are less common and less critical. For incumbents, the most effective form of contact is through the mails; the value of the frank is again apparent.

Voters interested in the campaign are generally more familiar with candidates, but not by a great amount. Other individual characteristics — attentiveness to the mass media, level of education, social class, whether or not the respondent shared the candidate's party affiliation — were not significantly related to familiarity in any of the equations, and so have been omitted. The R^2's are the multiple correlation coefficients (squared) and

TABLE 5.10
Sources of Voters' Familiarity with House Candidates, 1978

	Regression Coefficient	Standard Error	R^2
Dependent Variable:			
Familiarity with candidate			
Independent Variables:			
Incumbents ($N = 749$)			
Intercept	.47		
Contact:			
Personal	.10	.02	
Mail	.14	.02	
Mass media	.06	.03	.17
Family & friends	.08	.12	
Interest in campaigns	.06	.02	
Campaign expenditures	.02	.02	
Challengers ($N = 749$)			
Intercept	.08		
Contact:			
Personal	.05	.05	
Mail	.09	.03	
Mass media	.28	.03	.38
Family & friends	.16	.04	
Interest in campaigns	.09	.02	
Campaign expenditures	.08	.01	
Candidates for open seats ($N = 232$)			
Intercept	.26		
Contact:			
Personal	.01	.07	
Mail	−.01	.05	
Mass media	.30	.06	.29
Family & friends	.22	.07	
Interest in campaigns	.10	.05	
Campaign expenditures	.01	.03	

Source: NES/CPS American National Election Study, 1978.

measure the proportion of the variance in familiarity explained by all of the independent variables acting together. The proportion is greater for challengers (.38) and candidates for open seats (.29) than it is for incumbents (.17) in these equations.

TABLE 5.11
Campaign Expenditures and Familiarity with Candidates in the 1978
House Elections

	Regression Coefficient	Standard Error	R^2
Dependent Variable:			
Familiarity with candidate			
Independent Variables:			
Incumbents ($N = 749$)			
Intercept	.69		
Campaign expenditures	.02	.03	.00
Challengers ($N = 749$)			
Intercept	.20		
Campaign expenditures	.16	.01	.16
Candidates for open seats ($N = 232$)			
Intercept	.42		
Campaign expenditures	.08	.02	.06

Source: NES/CPS American National Election Study, 1978.

The Effects of Campaign Spending

The effects of campaign spending require special attention. They are masked somewhat in these equations because they operate, in part, indirectly. The more nonincumbents spend on a campaign, the more likely they are to have some kind of contact with voters, thus increasing their familiarity. The simple relationship between expenditures and familiarity is, in fact, a good deal stronger. The regressions of familiarity on expenditures are reported in Table 5.11. Campaign expenditures had no significant effect on how familiar voters were with incumbents in 1978 (or, for the most part, in previous elections for which requisite data are available[31]). Nor were incumbents' expenditures related to frequency of reported contacts or evaluations to any significant degree.

Campaign spending does have a substantial impact on how well voters know nonincumbents, particularly challengers; again,

---

[31] Jacobson, *Money*, pp. 145–157.

the evidence is entirely consistent with that from earlier elections. The more they spend, the better they are known and the more likely voters are to report contacts of all kinds and to offer evaluative comments about them. Interpreted crudely, the regression coefficient indicates that a challenger would have increased his level of familiarity by .16 on the scale for each $100,000 spent. The average challenger would have to have spent on the order of $320,000 to become as familiar as the average incumbent in 1978. This figure is well within the range of the commonly estimated monetary values of incumbency,[32] but it is of course more than what all but a handful of challengers were actually able to raise and spend.

These data help explain why campaign money is crucial to challengers and other nonincumbent House candidates. Without it, they are likely to remain obscure and so to be swamped by the opposition. They also explain why incumbents receive little measurable benefit from campaign expenditures. The campaign adds little to the prominence and affection they have gained prior to the campaign by cultivating the district and using the many perquisites of office.

Models of Voting Behavior in House Elections

How well voters know and like the candidates matters, finally, because familiarity and evaluations are directly related to the vote. The sets of regression equations reported in Tables 5.12 and 5.13 taken, respectively, from the 1978 and 1980 national election studies, suggest how this relationship works. More importantly, they make a fundamental point about the electoral effects of incumbency. The first equation in each table treats the vote choice as a function of party identification and incumbency status. Not surprisingly, these variables have a strong impact on the vote. The difference in the probability of voting Democratic in House elections shifts by .50 in 1978, by .39 in 1980, depending on whether the Democrat or the Republican is an incumbent.

The second equation in each table adds the candidate familiarity variables to the regression. The impact of incumbency

[32] Ibid., pp. 6–8.

TABLE 5.12

Regression Models of the Voting Decision in the 1978 House Elections

	Regression Coefficient	*Standard Error*	R^2
Dependent Variable:			
Respondent's vote ($N = 837$)			
Independent Variables:			
Equation 1			
Intercept	.50		
Party identification	.23	.01	.46
Democrat is incumbent	.24	.04	
Republican is incumbent	—.26	.04	
Equation 2			
Intercept	.54		
Party identification	.21	.01	
Democrat is incumbent	.14	.04	.50
Republican is incumbent	—.15	.04	
Familiarity with Democrat	.20	.04	
Familiarity with Republican	—.30	.04	
Equation 3			
Intercept	.58		
Party identification	.16	.01	
Democrat is incumbent	.06	.04	
Republican is incumbent	—.05	.04	.62
Familiarity with Democrat	.14	.04	
Familiarity with Republican	—.20	.04	
Likes something about Democrat	.20	.03	
Dislikes something about Democrat	—.19	.03	
Likes something about Republican	—.32	.03	
Dislikes something about Republican	.16	.03	

Source: NES/CPS American National Election Study, 1978.

is noticeably reduced; it would seem that a substantial portion of the incumbency advantage derives from the greater familiarity incumbents enjoy — the conventional hypothesis. But the third equation in each table suggests that the familiarity and, to

TABLE 5.13
Regression Models of the Voting Decision in the 1980 House Elections

	Regression Coefficient	Standard Error	R^2
Dependent Variable:			
Respondent's vote ($N = 733$)			
Independent Variables:			
Equation 1			
Intercept	.38		
Party identification	.22	.02	.37
Democrat is incumbent	.28	.06	
Republican is incumbent	—.11	.06	
Equation 2			
Intercept	.43		
Party identification	.21	.02	
Democrat is incumbent	.18	.06	.40
Republican is incumbent	—.05	.06	
Familiarity with Democrat	.24	.05	
Familiarity with Republican	—.28	.05	
Equation 3			
Intercept	.49		
Party identification	.15	.01	
Democrat is incumbent	.08	.05	
Republican is incumbent	—.03	.05	
Familiarity with Democrat	.12	.04	.58
Familiarity with Republican	—.16	.04	
Likes something about Democrat	.26	.03	
Dislikes something about Democrat	—.20	.03	
Likes something about Republican	—.31	.03	
Dislikes something about Republican	.25	.04	

Source: NES/CPS American National Election Study, 1980.

an even greater extent, incumbency variables are surrogates for voters' evaluations of the candidates. Each of the four evaluative variables derived from the likes/dislikes questions has a strong impact on the vote; something liked or disliked changes the likelihood of voting for the Democrat by from .16 to .32 independently of the other factors.

The effects of incumbency per se are greatly diminished; the regression coefficients are much smaller than in the first equation and do not reach conventional levels of statistical significance. The impact of the familiarity variables is cut in half.

The point is clear. Voters in 1978 and 1980 were not attracted by incumbency per se, nor did the incumbency advantage arise merely from greater renown. Of much greater importance were the very favorable public images members of the House acquired and the relatively negative images — if any — projected by their opponents.[33]

Evaluating Incumbents

The 1978 and 1980 election studies suggest that voters respond positively to House incumbents for a variety of reasons. Survey respondents were asked a number of general and specific questions about the incumbent's performance in serving the district and as a legislator in Washington. Tables 5.14 and 5.15 present data on some of the responses. The left-hand column in each table lists the percentage of voters who offered a relevant response to each question. For example, in 1978, 22 percent had asked the incumbent for assistance or information, received some reply, and therefore were able to indicate their level of satisfaction with it. The distribution of responses on this question shows that 65 percent of those who could respond on this dimension were very satisfied, and the right-hand column in the table indicates that 95 percent of those who were very satisfied with the incumbent's response voted for him. Only 3 percent were not at all satisfied with the response, and only 25 percent of these few voters voted for the incumbent.

It is apparent from the left-hand column that a large majority of voters could evaluate the incumbent's general job performance and could offer an opinion on whether or not the incumbent would be likely to help with a problem if asked to do so.

[33] Abramowitz, "Voting for U.S. Senator and Representative," p. 636; Thomas E. Mann and Raymond E. Wolfinger, "Candidates and Parties in Congressional Elections," *American Political Science Review* 74 (1980): 622–629; Hinckley, "House Re-elections and Senate Defeats," p. 456.

TABLE 5.14
Evaluations of the Incumbent's Performance and the Vote in the 1978 House Elections (in percentages; N = 749)

Relevant Responses	Evaluation of Performance		Distribution of Responses	Voting for Incumbent
90	*General Job Performance*	Very good	22	98
		Good	49	88
		Fair	25	61
		Poor	4	19
		Very poor	1	33
	District Services			
88	Expectations about incumbent's helpfulness in solving voter's problem	Very helpful	41	93
		Somewhat helpful	48	76
		Not very helpful	8	35
		It depends	3	81
21	Level of satisfaction with response to voter-initiated contact	Very satisfied	65	95
		Somewhat satisfied	28	80
		Not very satisfied	5	29
		Not at all satisfied	3	25
28	Level of friend's satisfaction with response	Satisfied	84	90
		Somewhat satisfied	9	88
		Somewhat dissatisfied	1	0
		Not satisfied	5	60

31	Could voter recall anything special incumbent did for the district?	Yes	31	86
		No	68	75

Voting and Policy

57	General agreement or disagreement with incumbent's votes	Agree	25	97
		Agree somewhat	49	87
		Neither agree nor disagree	16	63
		Disagree somewhat	7	52
		Disagree	4	25
16	Agreed or disagreed with vote on a particular bill	Agreed	69	94
		Disagreed	31	43
27	Which candidate would do a better job on most important problem?	Incumbent	80	98
		Challenger	20	5
16	Ideological proximity	Closer to incumbent	56	93
		Closer to challenger	44	23

Source: NES/CPS American National Election Study, 1978.

TABLE 5.15
Evaluations of the Incumbent's Performance and the Vote in the 1980 House Elections (in percentages; N = 681)

Relevant Responses	Evaluation of Performance		Distribution of Responses	Voting for Incumbent
78	*General Job Performance*	Approve strongly	49	95
		Approve, not strongly	39	77
		Disapprove, not strongly	6	22
		Disapprove strongly	6	7
	District Services			
86	Expectations about incumbent's helpfulness in solving voter's problem	Very helpful	38	91
		Somewhat helpful	50	70
		Not very helpful	10	36
		It depends	2	64
16	Level of satisfaction with response to voter-initiated contact	Very satisfied	67	93
		Somewhat satisfied	20	91
		Not very satisfied	4	50
		Not at all satisfied	9	20
21	Level of friend's satisfaction with response	Satisfied	80	84
		Somewhat satisfied	11	73
		Somewhat dissatisfied	1	50
		Not satisfied	8	46

23	Could voter recall anything special incumbent did for district?	Yes	23	83
		No	77	69

Policy and Ideology

22	Which candidate would do better job on most important problem?	Incumbent	75	97
		Challenger	25	8
25	Ideological proximity	Closer to incumbent	51	85
		Closer to challenger	49	29

Source: NES/CPS American National Election Study, 1980.

Fifty-seven percent were able to determine whether or not they generally agreed with the way the incumbent voted (the question was not asked in 1980). Fewer — from 16 to 31 percent — were able to respond in terms of more specific personal and district services, policy and voting, and ideological items. But more than 60 percent can respond in terms of at least *one* of them. That is, nearly two-thirds are able to evaluate incumbents in other than broad, general terms.

Reactions to incumbents, both general and specific, are over-whelmingly favorable. More than 70 percent of the voters offering relevant responses rated the incumbent's performance in office as good or very good in 1978; 88 percent approved mildly or strongly of his (or her) performance in 1980. About 90 percent in each year's sample thought he would be helpful or very helpful if they brought him a problem. Satisfaction with the incumbent's response to voter requests runs very high indeed; a large majority were "very satisfied," as were friends who had made similar requests. Nearly three-quarters of those responding generally agree with the incumbent's votes; 69 percent agree with his vote on a specific bill they recall. From 75 to 80 percent think he would do a better job dealing with what they perceive to be the most important problem facing the nation. Only on the ideological dimension is the incumbent's advantage not pronounced, and no more than a quarter of the voters can respond on this dimension.

The significance of these consistently positive responses is apparent from their association with the vote. On every dimension, the more positive the reaction to the incumbent, the more likely the respondent is to vote for him.[34] The sharpest differences are generally found on the more specific items; the most striking is that arising from respondents' judgments of which, if either, candidate would do a better job on what they think is the most important problem facing the country.

Naturally, respondents' assessments of incumbents on these dimensions are overlapping and interrelated. But they have a clear cumulative effect as well. If the positive and negative re-

---

[34] The only departures from monotonic relationships, in the job performance rating and level of friend's satisfaction in 1978, are based on six and twelve observations, respectively.

sponses are summed up, the greater the number of positive, the more frequently the respondent reports voting for the incumbent; the greater the number of negative responses, the more inclined respondents are to vote for the challenger. The relationship is strong and monotonic.[35]

Further evidence of how far House incumbents have succeeded in convincing voters that they serve them well can be gleaned from voters' responses to the questions about what they liked and disliked about the candidates in 1978 and 1980. As many as four responses were coded for each question. Their distribution by type for incumbents, challengers, and candidates for open seats is shown in Table 5.16. Things pertaining to job performance, experience, and district and individual services are mentioned most frequently as things liked about incumbents. They are mentioned much more rarely for nonincumbents — no surprise here — though more often for candidates for open seats, many of whom have held other elective offices, than for challengers. Most positive comments about nonincumbents have to do with personal characteristics (these are by no means unimportant for incumbents as well), which are, on the surface at least, empty of political content.

Given the importance traditionally attributed to party identification in guiding political judgments, it is remarkable how infrequently party is mentioned as a reason for liking or disliking a House candidate.[36] Party references tend to make up a larger share of the negative comments. So do references to ideology and policy. Efforts by House members to appeal for support on the basis of their personal virtues and services to the district and its inhabitants rather than on their party, ideology, or policy stances are evidently both wise and successful.

Taken as a whole, the evidence from the 1978 and 1980 election studies is that all of the things members of the House are purported to do in pursuit of reelection pay off. Individual voters respond, for example, to the advertising (familiarity, contacts), credit claiming (personal and district services), and position

[35] See Gary C. Jacobson, "Incumbents' Advantages in the 1978 Congressional Elections," *Legislative Studies Quarterly* 6 (1981):190.

[36] Party identification is also rather weakly related to the thermometer and likes/dislikes variables; the largest simple correlation in either year between any of these variables and party identification is .28.

TABLE 5.16

Voters' Mentions of Things they Liked and Disliked about 1978 and 1980 House Candidates (in percentages)

	Incumbents		Challengers		Candidates for Open Seats	
	1978	1980	1978	1980	1978	1980
Voters' Mentions of Things they Liked about Candidates						
Number of mentions	859	779	139	175	143	71
Percent of mentions, by type:						
Personal	39	31	58	46	55	59
Performance/experience	19	17	6	5	8	6
District service/attention	25	29	3	5	6	11
Party	1	3	4	6	4	1
Ideology/policy	12	15	27	25	18	21
Group associations	5	5	3	6	9	1

Voters' Mentions of Things
they Disliked about Candidates

Number of mentions	190	205	122	106	60	33
Percent of mentions, by type:						
Personal	40	42	44	34	42	30
Performance/experience	15	10	7	10	12	18
District service/attention	9	6	0	1	3	0
Party	7	7	7	5	5	0
Ideology/policy	22	32	42	49	35	39
Group associations	6	4	1	1	3	12
Number of Respondents	749	681	749	681	232	104

Note: Some columns do not sum to 100 because of rounding.
Source: NES/CPS American National Election Studies, 1978 and 1980.

taking (general and specific agreement with members' votes, ability to deal with the most important national problem) that David Mayhew identifies as the characteristic means by which incumbents pursue reelection.[37] And the home styles developed by the House members whom Fenno observed seem right on target. Fenno, recall, found that members typically work to project images devoid of partisan or even programmatic content, presenting themselves instead as trustworthy, hardworking people who deserve support for their experience, services, and personal qualities rather than for their political beliefs or goals.[38] They achieve this aim to a remarkable degree. Finally, it is also apparent that the electoral strategy of discouraging opposition before the campaign begins is both effective and effectively pursued. Most incumbent House members face obscure, politically inexperienced opponents whose resources fall far short of what it takes to mount a serious campaign.[39] It is obvious from the survey data how this would ease the incumbent's task of retaining voter support.

House incumbents appear to be doubly advantaged compared to their Senate counterparts. They are more highly regarded (compare the thermometer ratings in Table 5.6) and more likely to face obscure opponents (compare the figures on familiarity in Table 5.3). But these are not separate phenomena. Not only do popular incumbents discourage serious opposition, but in the absence of vigorous opposition, information that might undermine the incumbent's popularity seldom reaches voters.

Winning Challengers

The connection between the vigor of the challenge and the popularity of the incumbent is evident when we observe what happens when incumbents *are* seriously challenged. The most serious challenges are, by definition, the successful ones. Seven of the eighty-four incumbents whose districts were sampled by

[37] David R. Mayhew, *Congress: The Electoral Connection* (New Haven: Yale University Press, 1974), pp. 49–68.

[38] Richard F. Fenno, Jr., *Home Style: House Members in Their Districts* (Boston: Little, Brown, 1978), chapters 3 and 4.

[39] Jacobson, *Money*, chapters 3 and 5.

the 1980 election study were defeated.[40] Voters' responses to the survey questions about both challengers and incumbents in these districts are sharply different from those in districts where incumbents won. Table 5.17 reports the relevant data. Winning challengers are much better known by voters. More than half can recall their names and nearly all can recognize them and rate them on the thermometer scale. Incumbents are also better known in these races; a full-scale campaign generates somewhat more information all around. But their advantage over the challenger in familiarity is much smaller.

So is their advantage in voters' evaluations. Not only are winning challengers better known, they are also rated significantly higher on the thermometer scale. The incumbents they have defeated are rated significantly lower, so that the difference between the two is small and statistically indistinguishable from zero. A larger proportion of voters report things they like and do not like about winning challengers, but the increase in favorable statements is far greater. Voters can remember things they like about defeated incumbents as frequently as about winning incumbents, but they are much more likely to recall things they do not like about the former. The major differences, then, are in positive reactions to challengers and negative reactions to incumbents. As suggested in Chapter 4, effective challenges depend both on enhancing the challenger's standing and undermining that of the incumbent. Perceptions of House incumbents are by no means overwhelmingly positive when the stream of favorable messages from the incumbent's office is challenged by a substantial flow of critical information.

On general questions about job performance, losing incumbents fare almost as well as winning incumbents. Voters are just as likely to think they would be helpful if asked for assistance in solving a problem; 66 percent approve of their job performance, 20 percent disapprove, compared to figures of 69 percent and 9 percent for winning incumbents (with a larger proportion having no opinion on the latter). And voters are even more likely to remember something they have done for the district (44 percent, compared to 20 percent for winning incumbents),

---

[40] Eight were actually defeated, but one had just been elected in a special election and is best treated as a candidate for an open seat.

TABLE 5.17
Voters' Responses to Winning and Losing Challengers and Incumbents in the 1980 House Elections

	Challenger Won (n = 59)	Challenger Lost (n = 622)	Significance of Difference
Familiarity with the Candidates			
Recalled challenger's name	53	18	.001
Recognized name and could rate the challenger	92	51	.001
Neither	8	49	.001
Recalled incumbent's name	75	43	.001
Recognized name and could rate the incumbent	97	92	n.s.*
Neither	3	8	n.s.
Contact with the Challenger			
Any	81	40	.001
Met personally	9	4	n.s.
Received mail from challenger	37	13	.001
Read about challenger	59	24	.001
Saw challenger on television	51	21	.001
Family or friend had contact with challenger	20	9	.05
Evaluations of the Candidates			
Challenger's thermometer rating	58	51	.05
Incumbent's thermometer rating	60	67	.05

116

Likes something about challenger	39	13	.001
Dislikes something about challenger	15	11	n.s.
Likes something about incumbent	59	58	n.s.
Dislikes something about incumbent	46	18	.001
Ideology and Policy			
Most important problem:			
Challenger would handle better	24	4	.001
Incumbent would handle better	7	18	.05
Neither or none mentioned	69	78	n.s.
Ideological proximity:			
Closer to challenger	36	10	.001
Closer to incumbent	19	12	n.s.
Neither	46	78	.001

* Not significant.
Source: NES/CPS American National Election Study, 1980.

no doubt from having been reminded by the desperate incumbent. General performance and services to constituents do not appear to be sources of difficulty for them.

On ideological and policy dimensions, however, losing incumbents are in much worse shape than winning incumbents. There is a sharp reversal in voters' assessments of who would do the better job of dealing with the most important problem facing the country. This assessment (recall from Tables 5.14 and 5.15) is strongly related to the vote. The small advantage enjoyed by winning incumbents in ideological proximity to voters becomes a two-to-one disadvantage for losing incumbents. Furthermore, more than twice the proportion of voters can distinguish the two candidates on this dimension in districts where the incumbent lost. A larger proportion can also offer an opinion on which candidate would better handle the most important national problem, but the difference does not reach statistical significance.

As we would expect, voters are much more likely to report contacts with winning challengers than with losing challengers. Twice as many have had some kind of contact; the largest differences are in contacts through the mass media: newspapers, radio, and television. In fact, winning challengers are encountered as often as incumbents via these media; compare the figures in Table 5.8. The differences that remain between incumbents and winning challengers are in the modes of contact associated with holding the office over a period of years: personal and staff contacts and, of course, the mail.

It is no mystery why winning challengers reached so many more voters and were so much more familiar to them. They ran extraordinarily well-financed campaigns, spending, on the average, more than $330,000 each. In the six districts where comparisons can be made, they spent about three times as much as did the challengers who lost to these incumbents in 1978. The losing incumbents also increased their campaign spending from an average of $113,000 to $319,000, but since the marginal return on campaign spending by challengers is so much greater than on that by incumbents, the incumbents suffered a large net loss.[41]

---

[41] For a similar, but more detailed analysis of effects of strong challengers in 1980, see Malcolm E. Jewell, "The Political Environment of Congressional Elections," (Paper delivered during the Annual Meeting of the Southern Political Science Association, Memphis, November 5–7, 1981).

The 1980 elections made it clear that intensive cultivation of the district does not, by itself, guarantee reelection in the face of a vigorous challenge by a well-financed opponent. Working the district may be necessary for any incumbent whose positions are frequently at odds with district majorities, but it is not always sufficient to overcome stiff opposition. Several Democratic incumbents who had first been elected in 1974 to districts that had been Republican and who had held on in subsequent elections by providing services and publicizing themselves heavily were defeated. Notable among them was Andrew McGuire, who represented New Jersey's 7th District. McGuire, regularly spent three- or four-day weekends working the district. He held twenty-five "issue forums" on a variety of topics during his six years in office. He jogged through neighborhoods, stopping to talk with residents his advance men had talked into coming out. He had a large and effective district office staff and was a master at generating publicity about his activities. All this work was not enough to hold on against an attractive and articulate Republican (Marge Roukema) who spent $365,763 in a district where Reagan won 57 percent of the vote to Carter's 34 percent.[42]

Voting for House and Senate Candidates

In general, voters react to winning House challengers very much like they do to candidates for open seats and to Senate challengers.[43] And the limited comparative data available suggest that they react to losing House incumbents rather like they do to Senate incumbents (for example, their average ratings on the thermometer scale are about the same). Competitive challenges also make it possible for more voters to make ideological and policy distinctions between House candidates, again producing contests that are more like Senate elections, in which policy issues and ideology usually play a larger role.[44] This is further evidence that differences between House and Senate elections and among the varieties of House contests must be

[42] "Crack 'Outreach' Programs No Longer Ensure Reelection," *C.Q. Weekly Report* 39 (February 14, 1981):318.

[43] See Tables 5.3, 5.5, and 5.6.

[44] Abramowitz, "Voting for U.S. Senator and Representative," p. 638.

attributed primarily to the varying characteristics of House and Senate challengers and their campaigns.

To say this is to argue that differences among candidates, rather than differences in patterns of voting behavior, are what distinguish House and Senate elections. Identical equations representing House and Senate voting decisions in 1980 support this claim. The two equations in Table 5.18 regress the House

TABLE 5.18
Regression Models of House and Senate Voting in 1980

	Regression Coefficient	Standard Error	R^2
Dependent variable:			
Respondent's vote			
Independent variables:			
House of Representatives ($N = 733$)			
Intercept	.40		
Party identification	.15	.01	
Democrat is incumbent	.11	.05	
Republican is incumbent	.01	.05	.55
Familiarity with Democrat	.14	.04	
Familiarity with Republican	—.16	.04	
Democrat's thermometer rating/100	.80	.07	
Republican's thermometer rating/100	—.73	.08	
Senate ($N = 600$)			
Intercept	.45		
Party identification	.14	.02	
Democrat is incumbent	—.01	.03	
Republican is incumbent	—.05	.05	.55
Familiarity with Democrat	.22	.06	
Familiarity with Republican	—.23	.05	
Democrat's thermometer rating/100	.79	.07	
Republican's thermometer rating/100	—.68	.07	

Source: NES/CPS American National Election Study, 1980.

and Senate vote on party identification, incumbency, familiarity with the candidates, and candidate evaluations (using the thermometer ratings). The regression estimates are quite similar. The effects of party identification and candidate evaluations are scarcely distinguishable. With the other variables controlled, incumbency still influences House voters to a small degree but Senate voters not at all; the latter are slightly more sensitive to familiarity with the candidates. But these differences are small and easily overshadowed by the similiarities.

Issues in Congressional Elections

A broader implication of this argument is that congressional voters behave the way they do because politicians behave the way they do. We have seen, for example, how well voters' reactions to House incumbents fit the strategies they follow to win reelection. One explanation is that congressmen simply understand what appeals to voters and act accordingly. But the deviant cases (that is, challenger victories) and senatorial elections suggest that it does not work so simply. Voters react differently depending on the style and content, not to mention volume, of the appeals candidates make to them. Political strategies are based on assumptions about how individual voters operate; but voting behavior is constrained by the electoral context created by strategic decisions.

It is a classic illustration of mutual causation. And as Fiorina has pointed out, the converging patterns of electoral strategy and electoral behavior typical of congressional elections over the past two decades have conspired to crowd national political issues out of electoral politics.[45] Alert readers will have noticed that issues were hardly a prominent item in the discussion of voting behavior. The reason is that they show up so infrequently as having any measurable impact on individual voting in these election studies once other variables have been taken into account. Yet congressional elections have a profound impact on national policy, partly because the results are interpreted by

[45] Morris P. Fiorina, *Congress: Keystone of the Washington Establishment* (New Haven: Yale University Press, 1977).

politicians to reflect voters' preferences on policy matters. They can point to solid evidence that, *in aggregate*, congressional election results are highly sensitive to national issues and conditions to justify doing so. A resolution of this curious paradox is developed in the next chapter.

6
National Politics
and Congressional Elections

In the spring of 1981, at the behest of the Reagan administration, Congress began a drastic pruning of the social welfare system that had grown up over the preceding two decades. At the same time, taxes were reduced in a way that provided the largest cuts to people with the largest incomes. This combination of policies had the effect of redistributing income from poorer to wealthier citizens, reversing a political trend nearly fifty years old. Many of the programs scheduled for elimination first saw the light of day in the explosion of social welfare legislation that followed the 1964 elections. Left largely untouched were programs that had been enacted as part of the New Deal, which had itself represented a radical shift in national policy.

Each of these major changes in the direction of national policy was a product of the preceding congressional election. The New Deal, the Great Society, and Reagan's conservative counterattack on the welfare state all were made possible by a substantial net shift of congressional seats from one party to the other. The Reagan administration's victories were possible because the 1980 election had given Republicans control of the

Senate for the first time since 1952, and thirty-three more House seats, raising their share from 36 to 44 percent. Johnson's war on poverty went into high gear when Democrats increased their share of House seats from 59 percent to 68 percent in 1964; it was stopped cold when that share dropped back to 57 percent following the 1966 elections. The New Deal happened because the 1932 elections gave Roosevelt large and cooperative majorities in Congress, with reinforcements in 1934 and 1936.

The point of this brief historical excursion is that congressional elections are collective as well as individual events. When the wins and losses in all the separate contests are added up, the sums determine which party controls the House and Senate and with what size majority. The aggregate outcome also gives everyone in national politics some broad sense of what is on the public's mind. The raw numbers and their interpretation establish the opportunities and constraints that guide the direction of national policy for at least the next two years and often a good deal longer. The electoral politics of Congress may center on individual candidates and campaigns, but the collective results of congressional elections are what affect the course of national politics.

This is true not only in a specific and practical sense — the Democratic gains in 1964 leading directly to the adoption of the Medicare program, for example — but also more fundamentally. The possibility of responsible representative government in the United States depends on the capacity of congressional elections to influence the course of public policy. And this, in turn, is contingent on aggregate election results reflecting, in a meaningful way, the basic concerns of the public. How well they do this — how the millions of individual voting decisions in hundreds of distinctly individual contests combine to produce intelligible election results — is the main subject of this chapter.

Political Interpretations of Congressional Elections

Before the tools of survey research came into common use, politicians and political analysts had little problem interpreting aggregate congressional election results. It was widely understood that economic conditions (prosperity or recession, unemployment or price levels) and presidential politics (the popular standing of presidents or presidential candidates — influenced, to be sure, by economic conditions, but also by foreign triumphs or blunders, scandals, and other national issues) shaped the electoral prospects of congressional candidates. Thus it was possible to look at a set of figures like those in Table 6.1 and, with a little knowledge of contemporary events, make sense of them.

Republicans triumphed in 1946 because of economic dislocations and inflation brought on by postwar demobilization; Democrats made a comeback in 1948 behind Truman's spirited campaign and economic problems — strikes, rising prices — that

TABLE 6.1
Net Party Shift in House and Senate Seats in General Elections, 1946–1980

Year	House		Senate		President's Party*
1946	56	R	13	R	D
1948	75	D	9	D	D
1950	28	R	5	R	D
1952	22	R	1	R	R
1954	19	D	2	D	R
1956	2	D	1	D	R
1958	49	D	15	D	R
1960	22	R	2	R	D
1962	1	R	3	D	D
1964	37	D	1	D	D
1966	47	R	4	R	D
1968	5	R	6	R	R
1970	12	D	2	R	R
1972	12	R	2	D	R
1974	49	D	4	D	R
1976	1	D	0		D
1978	15	R	3	R	D
1980	33	R	12	R	R

Note: D indicates Democrats, R indicates Republicans.

* Denotes party of winning presidential candidate in presidential election years.

Sources: John F. Bibby, Thomas E. Mann, and Norman J. Ornstein, *Vital Statistics on Congress, 1980* (Washington, D.C.: American Enterprise Institute for Public Policy Research, 1980), table 1–3. Reprinted by permission. 1980 figures gathered by author.

could be blamed on the Republican Congress. Public dissatisfaction with the second Truman administration was clearly expressed in the 1950 and 1952 elections. A major recession took its toll of Republicans in 1958. The Goldwater debacle lengthened Johnson's coattails in 1964, the Republicans coming back in 1966 as discontent with Johnson's foreign policies spread. Republican congressional candidates were punished in 1974 for Nixon's Watergate sins and a recessionary economy. Inflation, Iran, and incompetence at the top of the ticket spelled disaster for Democrats in 1980. Plainly, it is not difficult to interpret congressional elections as national events controlled by national political conditions, and most political professionals do so routinely (the validity of such interpretations is another matter, of course).

Social scientists have examined the impact of national forces on congressional elections rather more systematically without undermining the conventional wisdom. A number of studies have investigated the effects of national economic conditions, variously measured, on the national division of the two-party vote for U.S. Representative.[1] Although the variety of approaches taken to the question (different economic indices, time periods, and control variables) has engendered important disagreements, most specifications produce the expected systematic relationship between the state of the economy and aggregate congressional election outcomes: the better the economy is performing, the better the congressional candidates of the president's party do on election day.

Edward Tufte took this work a step further by adding a meation years) or presidential candidates (in presidential election years) to the analysis. Tufte began with the familiar fact of political life that the president's party loses seats in midterm elections; the figures in Table 6.1 attest to it. The president's party

[1] Gerald H. Kramer, "Short-Term Fluctuations in U.S. Voting Behavior," *American Political Science Review* 65 (1971):131–143; G.J. Stigler, "General Economic Conditions and National Elections," *American Economic Review* 63 (1973):160–167; Francisco Arcelus and Allan H. Meltzer, "The Effects of Aggregate Economic Variables on Congressional Elections," *American Political Science Review* 69 (1975):1232–1239; Howard S. Bloom and H. Douglas Price, "Voter Response to Short-Run Economic Conditions: The Asymmetric Effect of Prosperity and Recession," *American Political Science Review* 69 (1975):1240–1254.

has not picked up seats in the House at midterm since 1934; on the average, it has lost thirty-one seats in postwar midterm elections. And most of the time, the party of the winning presidential candidate picks up congressional seats in a presidential election year (the postwar average is eighteen). The theory of surge and decline, discussed in the previous chapter, was an attempt to explain these phenomena as part of a single system. Not much support could be found for the theory in individual voting behavior. It also failed to explain the *size* of the midterm loss of the president's party, which varies from one to fifty-six House seats in postwar elections.

Tufte showed that the division of the congressional vote (and hence seats) in midterm (and, later, in on-year) elections was strongly and systematically related to simple measures of the economy and presidential popularity (or the relative popularity of the presidential candidates). He estimated the standardized vote loss by the president's party at the midterm (measured as the aggregate two-party vote subtracted from the average vote for the party in the previous eight congressional elections) as a function of (1) the percentage change in real disposable income per capita over the year preceding the election, and (2) the president's standing (percentage approving the way he is handling the job) in the Gallup Poll at the time of the election. His results are reported in Table 6.2.[2] They indicate that a difference of one percentage point in change in per capita income produces a difference of .6 percentage points in the standardized midterm vote for the president's party's congressional candidates, and a difference of 10 percentage points in the president's Gallup Poll approval rating is associated with a change of 1.3 percentage points in the vote.

Yearly change in real income has an even larger effect on the congressional vote in presidential election years, according to the second equation in Table 6.2. A one percentage point difference in the change in per capita income generates a 1.06 percentage point shift in the vote. The relative standing of the presidential candidates — measured by responses to the likes/

[2] Edward R. Tufte, *Political Control of the Economy* (Princeton: Princeton University Press, 1978), Tables 5–2 and 5–4; see also his "Determinants of the Outcomes of Midterm Congressional Elections," *American Political Science Review* 69 (1975):812–826.

TABLE 6.2
Tufte's Regression Models of Midterm and On-Year House Elections

	Regression Coefficient	Standard Error	R^2
Dependent Variable:			
Difference in percentage of House vote for party of the administration from an eight-year moving average			
Independent Variables:			
Midterm elections (1946–1974)			
Intercept	−10.74		
Yearly change in personal income	.62	.17	.83
Presidential popularity	.13	.04	
Presidential election years (1948–1976)			
Intercept	−3.98		
Yearly change in personal income	1.06	.44	.70
Net presidential candidate advantage, likes/dislikes	1.48	1.14	

Source: Edward R. Tufte, *Political Control of the Economy.* Copyright 1978 by Princeton University Press. Tables 5–2 and 5–4 adapted by permission of Princeton University Press.

dislikes questions in national election studies over the period covered — were also positively related to the congressional vote, but not at conventional levels of statistical significance.

Tufte's careful analysis left little doubt that economic conditions and presidential popularity are related to aggregate congressional election results. Furthermore, congressional electorates behave rationally; the party of the administration is held responsible for the performance of its president and of the economy. Tufte recognized that "many different models of the underlying electorate are consistent with electoral outcomes that are collectively rational," [3] but less cautious scholars have interpreted collective rationality to be a demonstration of equivalent individual rationality. The problem with this interpretation is

[3] Tufte, "Midterm Congressional Elections," p. 826.

that it is contradicted by almost all of the evidence from survey studies of individual voters.

The strong connection between aggregate economic variables and aggregate election results naturally inspired scholars to investigate the effects of economic conditions on the behavior of individual voters. At least four different kinds of economic variables might influence them: personal financial experiences and expectations; perceptions of general economic conditions; evaluations of the government's economic performance; and party images on economic policies.[4]

Most aggregate-level studies are based on the assumption that personal financial well-being is the primary criterion used by voters: "Rational voters are concerned with their real income and wealth."[5] The aggregate economic variables (change in real income per capita, percent unemployed) were chosen because they represent direct economic effects on individual citizens. But survey studies have turned up very little evidence that personal finances directly influence individual congressional voters. The occasional effects that do appear in some election years are generally indirect and much too weak to account for the robust relationships that Tufte and others find between national measures of economic conditions and election outcomes.[6]

Survey research does produce some evidence suggesting that economic conditions may influence the vote in one or more of the other ways. But the reported effects are almost always quite small and explain little additional variance in the vote once other variables (of the kind examined in the previous chapter) are

[4] M. Stephen Weatherford, "Social Class, Economic Condition, and Political Translation: The 1974 Recession and the Vote for Congress" (Paper delivered during the Annual Meeting of the Western Political Science Association, Portland, Oregon, March 22–24, 1979), pp. 3–7.

[5] Arcelus and Meltzer, "Congressional Elections," p. 1234.

[6] See Morris P. Fiorina, "Economic Retrospective Voting in American National Elections," *American Journal of Political Science* 22 (1978):426–443; Donald R. Kinder and D. Roderick Kiewiet, "Economic Discontent and Political Behavior: The Role of Personal Grievances and Collective Economic Judgments in Congressional Voting," *American Journal of Political Science* 23 (1979):495–527; M. Stephen Weatherford, "Economic Conditions and Electoral Outcomes: Class Differences in the Political Response to Recession," *American Journal of Political Science* 22 (1978):917–938 and "The 1974 Recession and the Vote for Congress."

taken into account. The behavior of individual voters does not conform to any simple model of economic rationality.

Survey findings about the electoral effects of voters' evaluations of presidents are somewhat more consistent with the aggregate evidence. Samuel Kernell found that, in midterm elections from 1946 through 1966, approval or disapproval of the president's performance was correlated with congressional preferences (with party identification controlled) and that disapproval had a greater effect than approval.[7] Other evidence from elections in the 1960s also showed presidential evaluations to influence congressional voting.[8] But studies of more recent midterm electorates find little to suggest that voters' feelings about the president swayed their congressional choice. Evaluations of Ford (in 1974) and Carter (in 1978) had no significant impact on the congressional vote.[9]

A related and more remarkable discovery is that reactions to Watergate did not appear to have much impact on individual voting behavior despite the heavy losses suffered by Republicans in 1974. Several studies found Watergate's effects to be indirect and unimpressively small,[10] although more sophisticated methods of analysis have turned up a significant link between voters'

[7] Samuel Kernell, "Presidential Popularity and Negative Voting: An Alternative Explanation of the Midterm Congressional Decline of the President's Party," *American Political Science Review* 71 (1977):44–66.

[8] Robert B. Arseneau and Raymond E. Wolfinger, "Voting Behavior in Congressional Elections" (Paper delivered during the Annual Meeting of the American Political Science Association, New Orleans, September 4–8, 1973); Candice J. Nelson, "The Effects of Incumbency on Voting in Congressional Elections, 1964–1974" (Paper delivered during the Annual Meeting of the American Political Science Association, San Francisco, September 2–5, 1975).

[9] Morris P. Fiorina, *Retrospective Voting in American National Elections* (New Haven: Yale University Press, 1981), p. 165; Gary C. Jacobson, "Congressional Elections 1978: The Case of the Vanishing Challengers," in *Congressional Elections*, eds. Louis Sandy Maisel and Joseph Cooper (Beverly Hills: Sage Publications, 1981), p. 238.

[10] M. Margaret Conway and Mikel L. Wyckoff, "Vote Choice in the 1974 Congressional Elections: A Test of Competing Explanations" (Paper delivered during the Annual Meeting of the Midwest Political Science Association, Chicago, April 21–23, 1977); Arthur H. Miller and Richard Glass, "Economic Dissatisfaction and Electoral Choice" (paper, Center for Political Studies, University of Michigan, 1977); Jack M. McLeod, Jane D. Brown, and Lee B. Becker, "Watergate and the 1974 Congressional Elections," *Public Opinion Quarterly* 41 (1977):181–195.

reactions to Ford's pardon of Nixon and the congressional vote choice.[11]

Various attempts have been made to account for the generally feeble connection between the economic and presidential popularity variables and individual congressional voting without abandoning the original premise of individual economic rationality; none has been convincing.[12] Fiorina has made the strongest case, arguing that personal economic experiences "affect more general economic performance judgments, both types of judgments feed into evaluations of presidential performance, and more general judgments, at least, contribute to modifications of party identification," which is known to be strongly related to the vote.[13] But even granting this complex process, the effects are a good deal weaker than the strong aggregate relationships would predict.

Presidential Coattails

The impact of voters' feelings about the presidential candidates on congressional voting is puzzling in a different way. Customarily, this has been discussed in terms of "coattail" effects. The term itself reflects the notion that successful candidates at the top of the ticket — in national elections, the winning presidential candidate — pull some of their party's candidates into office along with them, riding, as it were, on their coattails. Just how this works is open to much speculation. Perhaps the presidential choice has a direct influence on the congressional choice; people want to vote for candidates sharing their presidential favorite's party affiliation. Or perhaps both choices are influenced by the same set of considerations — for example, disgust with the failures of the current administration or delight with a party plaftorm to which both candidates are committed — and so move in the same direction. It is even conceivable that, on occa-

---

[11] Fiorina, *Retrospective Voting*, p. 165.

[12] See Gary C. Jacobson and Samuel Kernell, *Strategy and Choice in Congressional Elections* (New Haven: Yale University Press, 1981), pp. 12–13.

[13] Morris P. Fiorina, "Short- and Long-term Effects of Economic Conditions on Individual Voting Decisions," in *Contemporary Political Economy*, eds. D.A. Hibbs and H. Fassbender (Amsterdam: North Holland, 1981), pp. 73–100.

sion, support for the head of the ticket spills over from support for candidates for lower offices.

Regardless of the mechanisms operating, if a large number of fellow partisans are swept into office along with the president, political interpretation usually favors the traditional view embedded in the term itself. There is little apparent ambiguity in the absence of coattails, in any case; a presidential winner whose success is not shared by other candidates of his party did not have any.

The question of whether or not the president had strong coattails is of more than academic interest. Sheer numbers matter; administrations get more of what they want from Congress the more seats their party holds in the House and Senate. Roosevelt's New Deal, Johnson's Great Society, and Reagan's budget victories all depended on large shifts in party seats. Furthermore, members of Congress who believe that they got elected with the help of the president are more likely to cooperate with him, if not from simple gratitude then from a sense of shared fate; they will prosper politically as the administration prospers. Those convinced that they were elected on their own, or despite the top of the ticket, have much less incentive to be cooperative.

How such considerations affect congressional politics is discussed more thoroughly in the next chapter. The political significance of coattail effects (or the perception of them) is mentioned here because all of the aggregate evidence available indicates that they have become increasingly attenuated in recent years. Both cross-sectional (relating the presidential and congressional vote at the level of House districts) and time series (relating the national presidential and congressional vote over a series of election years) studies show a diminishing connection between presidential and congressional voting.[14] And if the presidential and congressional vote do not vary together, then meaningful coattail effects, however interpreted, do not exist.

Another way to see what has happened is to observe the data

[14] Walter Dean Burnham, "Insulation and Responsiveness in Congressional Elections," *Political Science Quarterly* 90 (1975):411–435; R. Lee Calvert and J. Arthur Ferejohn, "Presidential Coattails in Historical Perspective" (paper, California Institute of Technology, 1980); George C. Edwards III, *Presidential Influence in Congress* (San Francisco: W.H. Freeman, 1980), pp. 74–75.

in Table 6.3. The table lists the number and percentage of House districts that delivered split verdicts — majorities for the presidential candidate of one party, the House candidate of the other — in presidential election years from 1920 through 1980. The increase is obvious; the proportion of split results reached a peak of 44 percent in 1972, not far below the 50 percent mark that would be expected if no connection whatsoever existed and the pattern were random. In 1976 the proportion of split results dropped back to 29 percent, but other evidence suggested that

TABLE 6.3
Districts with Split Results in Presidential and Congressional Elections, 1920–1980

Year	Districts	Districts with Split Results[a]	
		Number	Percentage
1920	344 [b]	11	3.2
1924	356	42	11.8
1928	359	68	18.9
1932	355	50	14.1
1936	361	51	14.1
1940	362	53	14.6
1944	367	41	11.2
1948	422	90	21.3
1952	435	84	19.3
1956	435	130	29.9
1960	437	114	26.1
1964	435	145	33.3
1968	435	139	32.0
1972	435	192	44.1
1976	435	124	28.5
1980	435	147	33.8

[a] Congressional districts carried by a presidential candidate of one party and a House candidate of another party

[b] Prior to 1952 complete data on every congressional district are unavailable.

Sources: John F. Bibby, Thomas E. Mann, and Norman J. Ornstein, *Vital Statistics on Congress, 1980* (Washington, D.C.: American Enterprise Institute for Public Policy Research, 1980), Table 1–13. Reprinted by permission. 1980 data compiled by the author.

coattail effects had scarcely reasserted themselves. Of the 292 Democrats elected to the House that year, 270 received a larger share of the vote than Carter.[15] Few Democratic members of the 95th Congress had reason to think that Carter's electoral performance had anything to do with getting them elected. In 1980, the number of split results increased again to a level second only to 1972.

The detachment of congressional from presidential voting is another aspect of the trend that encompasses the decay of partisan ties and the rise of independent political entrepreneurs, most notably in the House. The larger electoral advantage enjoyed by House incumbents would have to be associated with weaker coattails unless their direction were reversed — the House incumbent attracting votes to his party's presidential candidate — and there is no evidence that this happened. Because the separation of presidential and congressional elections has such profound implications for national politics, it is worth considering the possibility that, despite the large proportion of split results reported in Table 6.3, the trend was reversed in 1980. Was Reagan's victory responsible for the Republican successes in House and Senate elections?

A simple test for the presence of coattail effects of some kind in 1980 can be made by adding a variable representing the presidential vote to the regression models presented in Table 5.18 of the previous chapter.[16] The results are reported in Table 6.4. They indicate that the presidential vote has a significant impact on the House and Senate vote even with the other variables controlled. The probability of voting for a Democratic House candidate is .07 greater for people who voted for Carter, .07 less for people who voted for Reagan, other things equal. In senatorial voting the likelihood of voting for the Democrat changes by .08 in either direction depending on the presidential vote. The addition of the presidential vote variable reduces the effect of party identification by about one-third (compare the equations in Table 5.18). But it does not reduce the effects of variables associated with the individual candidates and campaigns; they remain as large and important as before.

[15] *Congressional Quarterly Weekly Report* 36 (April 22, 1978):971–974.
[16] The presidential vote variable takes the value of 1 if the respondent voted for Carter; 0 if for Anderson or no one; −1 if for Reagan.

TABLE 6.4
Regression Models of Coattail Effects on House and Senate Voting in 1980

	Regression Coefficient	Standard Error	R^2
Dependent Variable:			
Respondent's vote			
Independent Variables:			
House of Representatives (N = 733)			
Intercept	.41		
Party identification	.11	.02	
Democrat is incumbent	.11	.05	
Republican is incumbent	.00	.04	.56
Familiarity with Democrat	.14	.04	
Familiarity with Republican	—.15	.04	
Democrat's thermometer rating/100	.78	.07	
Republican's thermometer rating/100	—.71	.08	
Presidential vote	.07	.02	
Senate (N = 600)			
Intercept	.48		
Party identification	.09	.02	
Democrat is incumbent	—.00	.03	
Republican is incumbent	—.05	.05	.56
Familiarity with Democrat	.21	.05	
Familiarity with Republican	—.22	.05	
Democrat's thermometer rating/100	.74	.07	
Republican's thermometer rating/100	—.66	.07	
Presidential vote	.08	.02	

Source: NES/CPS American National Election Study, 1980.

Another way to check for coattail effects is to observe the consequences of partisan defection in the presidential campaign on the congressional vote. The pattern for the 1980 elections is shown in Table 6.5. Clearly, people who voted for the other party's presidential candidate were a good deal more likely to vote for its House or Senate candidate as well; about half of the

TABLE 6.5
The Vote for Republican House and Senate Candidates, 1980, by Party Identification and Presidential Vote (in percentages)

Presidential vote	Party Identification					
	Republican		Pure Independent		Democrat	
Republican	76	(279)*	70	(37)	47	(71)
Democratic	61	(18)	22	(9)	20	(233)
Other or none	77	(30)	60	(15)	20	(41)
Republican	78	(224)	57	(28)	49	(59)
Democratic	50	(14)	36	(11)	13	(195)
Other or none	53	(19)	75	(12)	21	(38)

* Number of cases from which percentages were calculated.
Source: NES/CPS American National Election Study, 1980.

presidential defectors also defected in congressional elections, compared to less than 20 percent of the loyalists. About 80 percent of the defectors were Democrats voting for Reagan, so this pattern must have helped Republican congressional candidates. A simple calculation shows that, had presidential defections been divided equally and other things remained the same, the reported vote for House Republicans would have been 3 or 4 percentage points lower, for Senate Republicans about 2 percentage points lower.

The results of the 1980 survey indicate that nontrival coattail effects were present. But it is not convincing evidence that 1980 was very different from other recent election years. For even in 1972, when all the aggregate evidence showed little connection between presidential and congressional election results (Nixon won more than 60 percent of the vote, but Republicans gained only twelve seats in the House and *lost* two in the Senate), coat-

But another crucial consideration is whether it promises to be a good or bad year for the party. And that, it is widely believed, depends on national economic and political conditions. A booming economy and a popular president (or presidential candidate) are assumed to favor the party in power; economic problems and other national policy failings that are blamed on the administration are costly to its congressional candidates. *Exactly those things that politicians and political scientists looking at aggregate data believe influence congressional voters also guide the strategic decisions of potential candidates and contributors.*

This means that when the partisan outlook is gloomy, shrewd and ambitious politicians figure that the normally long odds against defeating an incumbent are even worse than usual and wait for a better day. People who supply campaign resources also decline to waste them trying to defeat incumbents they dislike and instead deploy them to defend their own favorite incumbents who may be in more trouble than usual.

Politicians of the other party, sensing that electoral tides are moving in their direction, view the chances of winning as better than usual, so more and better candidates compete for the nominations to challenge incumbents.[18] One thing that encourages them to make the race is easier access to campaign funds; contributors are also more willing to invest in challenges because political conditions seem favorable. Because the marginal effects of campaign spending are so much greater for challengers than for incumbents, the contrasting offensive and defensive contribution strategies do not simply cancel one another out; rather, they add to the vote totals of the party favored by national political conditions.

Thus when conditions appear to favor one party over the other, the favored party fields an unusually large proportion of formidable challengers with well-funded campaigns, while the other party fields underfinanced amateurs willing to run without serious hope of winning. In addition, incumbents of the disadvantaged party are marginally more likely to retire rather than face a tougher than usual campaign; the struggle for one more term may not be worth the effort.[19] This, too, means that the disadvantaged party will have relatively fewer strong candidates.

[18] Jacobson and Kernell, *Strategy and Choice,* p. 33.
[19] Ibid., pp. 49–59.

The choice between pairs of candidates across states and districts in an election year thus varies systematically with the strategic decisions of potential candidates and associated activists. These strategic decisions are systematically informed by perceptions of national political and economic conditions. Voters need only respond to the choice between candidates and campaigns at the local level to reflect, in their aggregate behavior, national political forces. It is not necessary for individual-level analogs of national forces — the voter's personal economic experiences and feelings about the president or presidential candidates — to influence the vote directly in order to affect the aggregate results. Some voters may be so influenced, but this kind of individual rationality is not required for the process to work. The intervening strategic decisions of congressional elites provide a mechanism sufficient to explain how national forces can come to be expressed in congressional election outcomes.

The logic of this explanation is straightforward enough; there is also a good deal of evidence for it. Politicians routinely sniff the political winds early in the election year; speculation about what will happen in the fall is a common feature of political news in January and February. Predictions are explicitly based on economic conditions and the public standing of the administration. Other information, from polls and special elections, for example, is also sifted for clues. Signs and portents are readily available, widely discussed, and taken seriously.[20]

They are also heeded. In 1974, for example, Watergate, recession, and the low standing of Nixon in the polls made it very difficult for Republicans to recruit good candidates at all levels. Republicans expected it to be a bad year and candidates and activists refused to extend themselves in a losing cause.[21] Democrats saw it as a golden opportunity, and an unusually large proportion of experienced candidates challenged Republican incumbents.[22]

[20] Ibid., pp. 27–29.

[21] "Running Hard in Watergate's Shadow," *C.Q. Weekly Report* 32 (February 16, 1974):353; "Southern Republicans: Little Hope this Year," *C.Q. Weekly Report* 32 (October 26, 1974):2959–2961.

[22] Linda L. Fowler, "Candidate Perceptions of Electoral Coalitions: Limits and Possibilities" (Paper delivered during the Conference on Congressional Elections, Rice University and the University of Houston, Houston, Texas, January 10–12, 1980), p. 11; Jacobson and Kernell, *Strategy and Choice*, p. 32.

Campaign contributors also respond to election year expectations. Some indication of this is found in the data in Table 6.7. Partisan differences in expenditures (which depend, of course, on contributions) are relatively small in years when national conditions did not seem to establish a clear favorite. In 1972, 1976, and 1978, Democratic and Republican challengers were able to raise and spend rather similar amounts of money. Republicans tended to spend somewhat more, but in none of these years is the difference greater than 25 percent. The same holds for incumbent Republicans and Democrats.

The 1974 and 1980 elections are rather different. In 1974, Democratic challengers typically spent three times as much as Republican challengers; they even outspent Democratic incumbents. Republican incumbents, on the defensive, spent 76 percent more than Democratic incumbents and more than four times as much as Republican challengers. In 1980 it was the

TABLE 6.7
Average Campaign Expenditures by House Candidates, 1972–1980, by Party and Incumbency Status

Year and Party	Incumbents	Challengers	Open Seats
1972			
Democrats	$49,249	$30,176	$96,762
Republicans	52,263	32,340	91,352
1974			
Democrats	46,331	59,331	103,091
Republicans	81,436	20,744	79,903
1976			
Democrats	79,100	44,646	144,060
Republicans	90,184	55,484	97,687
1978			
Democrats	111,424	70,947	212,671
Republicans	138,765	73,043	192,514
1980			
Democrats	166,190	68,767	189,022
Republicans	190,729	111,149	204,511

Note: Includes candidates with major party opposition only.

Source: Compiled by author from data supplied by Common Cause (1972 and 1974) and the Federal Election Commission (1976–1980).

Republicans' turn to go on the offensive and the Democrats' to try to save incumbents. Republican challengers outspent Democratic challengers by more than 60 percent; Democratic incumbents spent 2.4 times as much as Democratic challengers. The main difference between spending patterns in the two years is that favored Republican incumbents spent relatively large amounts of money in 1980; the reason seems to be that Republican and conservative groups raised vast amounts of money and all Republicans benefitted. That aside, the patterns could hardly be clearer. Campaign contributions — and hence expenditures — were sharply responsive to perceived political trends in 1974 and 1980.

Credible campaign finance data do not exist for elections prior to 1972, so it is not possible to see how well these patterns hold up over time. But it is possible to show that variations in the relative quality of each party's candidates are strongly related to national conditions and aggregate election results in the way necessary for the explanation to be valid. Consider the regression equations in Table 6.8. Equation 1 indicates that the aggregate quality of each party's challengers, measured as the percentage of them who have held elective office, has a substantial and statistically significant impact on the aggregate congressional vote (outside the South[23]) in elections from 1946 through 1980. In the second equation, the two independent variables are combined into a single index of relative challenger quality (the difference in the two percentages) and this, along with another indicator of a party's relative advantage or disadvantage in candidate quality — the percentage of incumbents running who belong to the party — is regressed on the aggregate congressional vote. Again, both variables have a large and significant impact on the congressional vote.

Plainly, the relative quality of each party's candidates is quite strongly related to how well the party does in the election. A difference of 10 points between the percentage of Democratic and Republican challengers who have won elective office is as-

[23] The South is excluded from the analysis because for at least the first half of this time period, the Republican Party was not competitive in most Southern districts (the South is defined as the eleven states of the Confederacy). Political strategies would of course be quite different where the real competition takes place in a primary election.

TABLE 6.8
The Quality of Candidates, and Aggregate Congressional Election Results, 1946–1980

	Regression Coefficient	Standard Error	$\bar{R}^2$
Dependent Variable:			
Democrat's percentage of two-party House vote			
Independent Variables:			
Equation 1			
Intercept	49.0		
% of Democratic challengers who have held elective office	.36	.12	.63
% of Republican challengers who have held elective office	−.22	.09	
Equation 2			
Intercept	44.2		
Difference in % of challengers who have held elective office (% Democrats − % Republicans)	.28	.04	.76
% of incumbents who are Democrats	.12	.04	

Note: $\bar{R}$ is the multiple correlation coefficient adjusted for small number of cases.
Source: Data compiled by author.

sociated with a difference of 2.8 percent of the vote; the maximum difference over these years was 24.7 in 1974, which is associated with a 6.9 percentage point advantage for Democrats. But just as clearly, these equations leave open the question of whether variations in the vote are actually *produced* by differences in the quality of candidates. It is entirely conceivable that the causal sequence runs in the opposite direction: (accurate) expectations about what will happen in the fall produce variations in the kinds of candidates the party fields. Assuming strategic rationality and accurate prediction, this should, indeed, occur. The connection is unmistakable; the central question remaining is the degree to which strategic politicians simply ride a favorable electoral tide and the degree to which their decisions and actions swell the tide.

This is a difficult question to answer. Certainly recent survey studies of congressional elections suggest that the individual candidates and campaigns matter much more to voters than national issues; therefore, strategic political choices should be instrumental in generating aggregate election results. Some indirect evidence of this is provided by a reexamination of Tufte's model. Tufte calculated the change in per capita income from yearly data, which are actually measured from July 1 of one year to July 1 of the next. But if economic conditions as directly experienced by voters at the time of the election are what influences the vote, measures taken closer to election day should show an even stronger connection with election results. Quarterly income data are available to test this notion. And it is also possible to measure the impact of presidential popularity ratings expressed earlier in the year on what happens at the midterm. Equation 1 in Table 6.9 is a revised version of Tufte's equation, adding the 1978 election and using voting results outside the south only. It matches the original findings and fits the data about as well as Tufte's model. Equations 2 through 6 estimate the effects of income changes[24] and presidential popularity[25] in each of five periods beginning with the last quarter of the year preceding the election and ending with the fourth quarter of the election year.

Separated in this way, the data reveal a striking pattern. The economy and presidential popularity together have their strongest impact on midterm congressional elections when they are measured in the *first quarter* of the election year. The coefficient on income change is larger, and its standard error smaller, in

[24] Data are from U.S. Department of Commerce, Bureau of Economic Analysis, *National Income and Product Accounts of the United States, 1929–74: Special Tables,* pp. 68–73; later figures are from the Bureau's *Survey of Current Business.*

[25] Presidential popularity is measured as the average percentage of Gallup Poll respondents who approve of the president's performance in surveys taken during the quarter. The number of surveys per quarter ranges from one to six; the most common number by far is three. The measure for the fourth quarter of the election year is Tufte's.

TABLE 6.9
Midterm Congressional Elections Revisited

| | Independent Variables | | | |
	Intercept	Change in Personal Income	Presidential Popularity	$\bar{R}^2$
Dependent Variable:				
Difference in percentage of House vote for party of the administration from eight-year moving average				
Equations:				
Tufte's model (revised)	−9.5	.81	.104	.73
4th quarter of year		(.18)*	(.054)	
preceding election year	−8.1	.56	.078	.16
		(.32)	(.070)	
1st quarter	−9.4	.79	.092	.81
		(.15)	(.032)	
2nd quarter	−8.1	.70	.087	.72
		(.17)	(.044)	
3rd quarter	−6.8	.72	.062	.67
		(.21)	(.048)	
4th quarter	−8.6	.60	.096	.37
		(.26)	(.081)	

* Standard error.

Note: $\bar{R}$ is the multiple correlation coefficient adjusted for small number of cases.

Sources: Income data are from U.S. Department of Commerce, Bureau of Labor Statistics, *National Income and Product Accounts of the United States, 1929–74: Special Tables,* pp. 68–73; later figures are from the Bureau's *Survey of Current Business.* Presidential popularity data are from Gallup Polls.

this quarter than in any other. The effect of presidential popularity measured in the first quarter is second only to its effect measured in the fourth quarter, and in the fourth quarter equation, its coefficient does not approach the customary criterion for statistical significance (being at least twice as large as its standard error) and so cannot be considered a sufficiently precise estimate to be taken seriously. The first quarter equation matches Tufte's model most closely. This pattern makes no sense if these variables are taken to be summary measures of individual attitudes and economic circumstances that directly affect the voting decision.[26] But if they are taken to represent information used by potential candidates and their potential supporters to make strategic decisions which ultimately influence election results by generating the choices presented to voters, they work exactly as expected. The strongest effects of national conditions on congressional elections are, by these equations, clearly indirect.

This exercise is completed by adding the measure of challenger quality to the equations estimating the midterm election outcomes; the results are reported in Table 6.10. This variable is closely related to the aggregate vote no matter when the other variables are measured. Presidential popularity no longer has a significant impact in any of the equations. The effect of the income variables is reduced in all of the equations, but it remains significant in all but the fourth quarter. Interestingly, it continues to have its greatest impact on election outcomes when measured in the first quarter of the election year. Early-year economic conditions are not, by this evidence, registered entirely through their effects on candidate decisions. Perhaps the variable works as an indirect measure of other strategic decisions (revealing the conditions that guide those decisions) which independently contribute to election outcomes by influencing the choices ultimately presented to voters. Potential challengers are not the only important strategic activists, after all. In any case, these two variables explain, statistically, virtually all the variation in the midterm congressional vote in the first-quarter equation. This does not change if presidential popularity is dropped from the analysis.[27]

A similar analysis of presidential election year data does not produce such clearcut results. If only candidates of the party

[26] Because the income figures are an average for the three months of the quarter, the actual figure reported tends to be closest to that of the middle of the period; for the fourth quarter, that puts it in mid-November, closest to election day of any income measure.

[27] See Gary C. Jacobson, "Strategic Politicians and Congressional Elections, 1946–1980" (Paper delivered during the Annual Meeting of the American Political Science Association, New York, September 3–6, 1981), Table 4.

opposing the administration are considered, then the midterm pattern is repeated almost exactly; the quality of the opposition's challengers is strongly related to the congressional vote no matter what quarter the economic variable is measured, and that variable and the two together have their strongest effect in the first-quarter equation.[28] But the president's party's challengers appear to be less strategic, and their aggregate quality is only weakly related to the aggregate vote (although in the predicted direction). On the other hand, the relative quality of both parties' challengers is significantly related to their relative proportion of challenger *victories*, even in presidential election years.[29]

Reviewing the evidence as a whole, it seems certain that the political strategies of congressional elites are a response to national forces and help to express them in aggregate election results. Complete evidence — on candidates, campaign finances, and voting behavior — is available only for the most recent decade, and it is for this period that the strongest case can be made that elite strategies provide the essential connecting link between national forces and congressional election outcomes.

It is very likely that in earlier electoral periods, national forces influenced voters more directly. It would be difficult to argue, for example, that many congressional voters in 1932 or 1934 or 1936 were not responding directly to their economic experiences during the Depression or to their feelings about Franklin Roosevelt. Individual congressional candidates were important only insofar as they were committed to a position for or against the New Deal. Elections like these were, of course, the source of the conventional wisdom about the effect of national forces on the fates of congressional candidates. Shrewd politicans would be well-advised to adjust their career strategies to take advantage of favorable national tides and to avoid contrary currents.

If, over the years, individual candidates and campaigns became comparatively more important and national forces less so, politicians would not necessarily abandon their traditional strategies. They would, rather, continue to respond strategically to national trends because, increasingly as a consequence of their

[28] Ibid., Table 7.
[29] Ibid., Table 8.

TABLE 6.10
The Effects of Quality of Challengers, Personal Income, and Presidential Popularity in Midterm Congressional Elections, 1946–1978

		Independent Variables			
	Intercept	Difference in % of Challengers Who Have Held Elective Office	Change in Personal Income	Presidential Popularity	R^2

Dependent Variable:

Difference in percentage of House vote for party of the administration from eight-year moving average

Equations:

	Intercept	Difference in % of Challengers Who Have Held Elective Office	Change in Personal Income	Presidential Popularity	R^2
4th quarter of year preceding election year	−.5	.22 (.07)*	.18 (.24)	−.017 (.055)	.65
1st quarter	−3.9	.15 (.03)	.56 (.09)	.016 (.022)	.96
2nd quarter	−2.6	.16 (.04)	.48 (.11)	.002 (.005)	.91

3rd quarter	−1.5	.17 (.06)	.48 (.16)	−.019 (.043)	.85
4th quarter	−3.3	.18 (.08)	.31 (.23)	.024 (.080)	.68

* Standard error.

Note: R is the multiple correlation coefficient adjusted for the small number of cases.

Sources: Candidate data are from Congressional Quarterly's special preelection issues of *Congressional Quarterly Weekly Report* and the Congressional Staff Directory's *Election Index* for elections from 1960 through 1980; data for earlier election years are from newspaper archives; some data are missing from earlier periods, but no more than 5 percent of the cases in any year. They were collected under National Science Foundation Grant SES 80-07577 as part of a continuing research project; income and presidential popularity data are from the sources listed in Table 6.9.

own strategic choices (and those of other congressional activists), their expectations about election outcomes continued to be realized. At the extreme, their expectations could come to be based on false assumptions, their prophecies wholly self-fulfilling. National economic and political conditions might affect congressional elections only because congressional elites expect them to do so.

There is no reason to think that this point has yet been reached, although the trend has been moving in that direction. Electoral prophecies are, at present, clearly self-reinforcing, but not entirely self-fulfilling. But any further weakening of the link between voters' responses to national forces and their voting decisions threatens to undermine the capacity of the electorate to hold politicians collectively responsible for their performance. Politicians are not fools; it is hard to believe that they would not notice if the connection were completely severed. And if they perceived no connection, their strategic behavior would no longer provide the mechanism through which the electorate acts as, in V.O. Key's phrase, a "rational god of vengeance and reward." [30]

The 1980 Elections

The 1980 elections certainly seemed to confirm the idea that national issues affect congressional election results. Republicans picked up twelve seats in the Senate, thirty-three in the House; it is tempting to conclude that Democratic congressional candidates were punished for the failings of the Carter administration, sharing the blame for an unprecedented combination of high inflation and high unemployment. But a closer look at what happened in 1980 again underlines the crucial role of individual candidates and campaigns and gives little ground for thinking that strong, direct links between national political forces and individual voting decisions have been reforged.

The first thing to notice is how much better Republicans did in Senate than in House campaigns. They defeated 46 percent of the incumbent Senate Democrats running compared to 11

[30] V.O. Key, Jr. (with the assistance of Milton Cummings), *The Responsible Electorate* (Cambridge: Harvard University Press, 1966), p. 7.

percent of those running in House elections. This difference cannot be explained by coattail effects or other national forces; it is, rather, a consequence of the strategic decisions of politicians and their supporters.

Consider: of the nine successful Republican Senate challengers, four were present members of the House and a fifth had been until 1978. Two others had held statewide office as attorneys general. Another was the state party chairman. The only political neophyte, John P. East of North Carolina, benefitted from the lavish campaign resources put at his disposal by his patron, Senator Jesse Helms. All of them were, at the very least, adequately financed.

Most of the ten incumbent Democrats who avoided defeat faced much weaker opponents. One was unopposed and five had challengers who had been written off as hopeless by their own partisans.[31] These Democrats actually increased their share of the vote by an average of 3.2 percentage points over 1974 in the four cases where the comparison can be made. The other four managed to turn back stiff challenges despite a substantial loss of votes from 1974. The shift to Republicans in the Senate was by no means uniform, but depended heavily on particular challengers and campaigns.[32]

The same is true of House elections. Republicans did not do so well in them simply because they fielded relatively fewer attractive challengers with adequately financed campaigns. No explanation of House elections relying on national forces can explain why 77 of the 186 Democratic House incumbents who faced Republican opposition in both 1978 and 1980 actually *improved* on their 1978 vote or why 29 of the 113 incumbent Republicans did worse than in 1978. The mean Republican vote gain was a little more than three percentage points; but its standard deviation was even larger than it has been in other recent elections, about 11 percentage points.

A more detailed look at winning Republican challenges indicates that success was contingent upon particular candidates

[31] "The Outlook: Senate, House, and Governors," *C.Q. Weekly Report* 38 (October 11, 1980):2986–3086.

[32] The correlation coefficient, squared, between the Republican presidential and senatorial votes (two-party) was only .23 in 1980; only 23 percent of the variance of the vote in both elections was shared.

and campaigns. The data in Table 6.11 show plainly that they did not simply ride a favorable tide. The table lists the percentage of winning Republican challengers according to two variables: whether or not the seat was marginal, and whether or not a strong challenge was mounted against the incumbent. Marginal seats are defined as those which the Democratic incumbent won in 1978 with less than 60 percent of the two-party vote. Strong challenges are those in which the challenger spent more than $100,000 on the campaign.

The strength of the challenger's candidacy is obviously the crucial variable. One-third of the strong candidacies were successful; only 2.1 percent of the others defeated incumbents, and Abscam indictments were behind two of the three cases involved. Marginal incumbents did attract more serious challenges (58 percent, compared to 19 percent for nonmarginal incumbents), which is just what our understanding of political career strategies would lead us to expect. But strong challengers actually had a higher rate of success in *nonmarginal* districts. Remarkably, no Republican challenger who did not spend at least $100,000 was able to take a marginal seat from a Democratic incumbent.

TABLE 6.11
Winning Republican Challengers, 1980 House Elections (in percentages)

	Democratic Incumbent					
Republican Challenger	Marginal		Nonmarginal		Total	
Strong challenge	29.0	(38) *	48.2	(27)	36.9	(65)
Weak challenge	0.0	(27)	2.6	(117)	2.1	(144)
Total	16.9	(65)	11.1	(144)	12.9	(209)

* Number of cases from which percentages were calculated.

Note: Marginal seats are those in which the Democratic incumbent won less than 60 percent of the two-party vote in 1978. Strong challenges are those in which the challenger spent at least $100,000.

Source: Campaign spending data are from Alan Ehrenhalt, ed., *Politics in America: Members of Congress in Washington and at Home* (Washington, D.C.: Congressional Quarterly Press, 1981).

Not every strong Republican challenge succeeded, of course. The point is that almost every winning challenge involved a formidable individual campaign which might easily have been effective even without Reagan's victory or Carter's unpopularity. At the very least, successful challengers had positioned themselves to take full advantage of whatever help the national campaigns and other national forces might bestow, and this was a necessary condition of their success.

Some reasons why Republicans would mount a larger proportion of formidable campaigns in Senate races were offered at the end of Chapter 4. Incumbent senators are, on several grounds, more vulnerable than House incumbents, and Senate seats are more desirable than House seats. In 1980, Republican activists — party politicians, political action committees, and other suppliers of campaign resources — very clearly concentrated their efforts on Senate challenges. Some evidence of this is in Table 6.12. Early party expenditures were concentrated in Senate races, and the largest share of the money went to challengers and candidates for open seats. The strategy here was clearly offensive: designed to take seats from the opposition, without much concern for protecting incumbents (they did not seem to need the help). The pattern of early expenditures for Republican House candidates is quite different, with incumbents getting most of the help and the average amount spent being relatively small. Challengers were treated relatively better later in the campaign, but early money is especially important for getting a serious campaign off the ground.

Early Democratic expenditure strategies were plainly defensive, even more so in Senate than in House campaigns. Notice also that the average amounts spent for the Democratic candidates are much lower. A similar pattern is evident in the early campaign contributions of political action committees whose partisan orientation is sharply defined. Observe the data in Table 6.13. Labor PACs, which contribute overwhelmingly to Democrats, concentrated on defending threatened incumbents. Business and conservative PACs strongly preferring Republicans gave most of their funds to challengers.

These contrasting contribution strategies are just what we should expect when congressional activists believe that national forces obviously favor one party's candidates. They are also

TABLE 6.12
Early Party Spending in the 1980 Congressional Elections

Party	Receipts	Expenditures	Share Given to		
			Incumbents	Challengers	Open Seats
Republicans					
National Republican Senatorial Committee	$10,444,980	$3,275,887	7.0%	59.8%	33.2%
National Republican Congressional Committee	12,952,900	1,981,150	60.9	18.8	20.3
Republican National Committee	34,013,904	581,792	13.3	54.5	32.2
Democrats					
Democratic Senatorial Campaign Committee	438,958	363,000	74.8	14.2	11.0
Democratic Congressional Campaign Committee	1,383,211	334,244	59.9	18.9	21.2
Democratic National Committee	6,015,352	374,174	56.8	20.9	22.3

Source: FEC Reports filed from January 1, 1979 through September 30, 1980. The figures for the National Republican Congressional Committee include the period through August 30, 1980, only.

TABLE 6.13
Early Campaign Contributions of Selected Partisan Political Action Committees, 1980

Political Action Committee	Contributions	Republicans	Democrats	Share Given to Incumbents	Challengers	Open Seats
AFL-CIO COPE	$ 748,920	3.4%	96.6%	57.1%	23.5%	19.4%
United Auto Workers	1,359,676	1.4	98.6	67.1	17.5	15.4
Business-Industry PAC	129,620	90.2	9.8	24.2	52.7	23.1
Gun Owners of America PAC	122,526	92.8	7.2	9.2	67.1	23.7
National Conservative PAC	128,169	92.3	7.7	19.6	56.7	23.7

Source: FEC Reports filed through October 15, 1980. Figures do not include independent expenditures.

strategies that contribute to the results anticipated by the activists. The favored party — the Republican in this case — mounts a larger proportion of strong challenges and thereby does noticeably better on election day, just as expected.

This is not to deny that national forces — economic conditions, public reactions to the presidential candidates — were at work in 1980. But the strategies pursued by political elites, in light of expectations about the likely course of political events given the national forces, were essential to the final results. Individual candidacies still dominate the process; few Republicans who did not thoroughly prepare the ground were swept into office.

For now, at least, although national issues may not count for a great deal in individual voting decisions, they do influence the strategic decisions of congressional elites. Elite strategies generate choices across states and districts that systematically reflect national forces. Responding to candidates and campaigns, voters respond systematically, if indirectly, to national forces as well. Collectively, congressional elections hold the administration's party responsible for the general state of economic and political life.

But the capacity of congressional elections to hold administrations and parties responsible has clearly decreased in recent years. One obvious reason is the greater incumbency advantage, which, among other things, insulates members from national forces. The largest aggregate House vote shift since the Second World War was 7.9 percentage points; with more than 70 percent of incumbents routinely winning with more than 60 percent of the vote, the effects of even large national swings are dampened. Another is the dissociation of presidential and congressional voting, exemplified by the decline of presidential coattails. Voters who choose presidents and members of Congress more or less independently of one another do not encourage collective responsibility; individual congressmen can escape the consequences of the collective failures of an administration and need not share their president's fate (and, therefore, interests). How this and other aspects of congressional election politics affect the performance of Congress as an institution and of the national government itself is the subject of the next chapter.

7

Elections and
the Politics of Congress

Congressional elections matter because the U.S. Congress matters. Though not immune from the trend toward executive dominance of politics that is characteristic of modern democracies, Congress has retained so much of its institutional autonomy that an astute political scientist, Morris P. Fiorina, could plausibly consider it the "Keystone of the Washington Establishment."[1] Congress performance as an institution therefore has a profound effec on how and how well we are governed. The workings of Congress, its strengths and weaknesses as a governing institution, are in turn intimately connected to how its members win and hold office.

This chapter examines how the system of electoral politics depicted in the first six chapters affects the workings of the House and Senate. Its central theme is the inherent tension between individual and collective pursuits. Congressional office is

[1] Morris P. Fiorina, *Congress: Keystone of the Washington Establishment* (New Haven: Yale University Press, 1977).

an individual franchise; members win and hold seats largely through their own personal efforts. But it is what Congress does collectively that makes membership in it worth winning. The institutional strength of Congress is, for its members, a collective good. All members benefit from belonging to a powerful and effective legislative body. They enjoy the benefit, however, regardless of whether or not they contribute to its achievement. The electoral needs of individual members and the work required to make Congress an effective governing body often generate conflicting demands. The potential cost of ignoring the former is specific and personal: loss of office. The potential cost of ignoring the latter is diffuse and collective: an imperceptible marginal weakening of authority. It is obvious where the balance of incentives lies. The problem is that, as David Mayhew puts it, "efficient pursuit of electoral goals by members gives no guarantee of institutional survival. Quite the contrary. It is not too much to say that if all members did nothing but pursue their electoral goals, Congress would decay or collapse."[2]

Congress has not collapsed. Its members — most of them, anyway — have other goals besides reelection. Holding office may be essential to the achievement of these other ends, but it is only worth the effort because it allows their pursuit. Richard Fenno has identified making good public policy and earning influence and respect in Washington as the most important of these goals; Congress' institutional performance is crucial to both.[3] Members have therefore developed and supported institutional structures and processes designed to harness the individual energies of its members to collectively important ends. These institutional devices necessarily reflect their origins. They must cope with conflicting demands for collective effectiveness and individual autonomy, strong leadership and broad participation, coherent policy and particularized benefits. It is not surprising that they often fail to work as expected, are subject to continual criticism from one quarter or another, and are altered in a fit of reform from time to time.

[2] David R. Mayhew, *Congress: The Electoral Connection* (New Haven: Yale University Press, 1974), p. 141.
[3] Richard F. Fenno, Jr., *Congressmen in Committees* (Boston: Little, Brown, 1973), p. 1.

Mayhew has written a brilliantly lucid analysis of how the internal workings of Congress reflect the demands of electoral politics and the need to deal with their destructive tendencies.[4] Much of what follows in this chapter is drawn from his work. Such a well-told story need not be repeated in detail; I therefore touch on only enough of his analytical points to suggest the structure of his argument. One aspect of congressional organization intimately tied to electoral politics — the office, staff, travel, and communications resources enjoyed by all members — has already been discussed (see Chapter 3) and need not be mentioned further. I begin here with brief consideration of three of Congress' most important institutional components: the committee system, the congressional parties, and the budgetary process. Mayhew's book was completed in the early 1970s. Each of these components has changed a great deal since then. It is a tribute to Mayhew's perspicacity that these changes, far from undermining his analysis, are best understood in its light.

The Committee System

Most legislative activity and all administrative oversight — two major institutional functions of Congress — take place in committees and subcommittees. The House and Senate are thoroughly decentralized bodies. Activity and authority in Congress are decentralized to encourage *specialization*. The number, variety, and complexity of issues that come before Congress make it essential that members develop specialized knowledge of specific policy areas. This requires a division of labor. Each member needs to focus his or her legislative attention narrowly, because none has the time or energy to become thoroughly knowledgeable about more than a few complex issues and questions. The alternative to developing specialized expertise in Congress is surrender of power to experts in the White House, the administrative agencies, or the private sector. A decentralized system of standing committees with fixed jurisdictions is Congress' organizational strategy for survival as a significant policy-making institution.

[4] Mayhew, *Electoral Connection,* chapter 2.

The committee system certainly serves the collective interests of congressmen. But as it actually functions, it also serves the electoral needs of individual members and, at the same time, works to limit the damage this may do to the collective performance of Congress. Some committees do little legislative work while providing a platform for position taking: making statements and symbolic gestures aimed at pleasing constituent groups. Committees charged with investigating subversives, corruption, or cost overruns on defense contracts are examples; they permit members to speak out bravely against subversion, corruption, and waste. So are committees dealing with issues having a strong ideological tinge, like the House Education and Labor Committee or those dealing with foreign affairs. Other committees generate individual benefits for specific states, districts, groups, even individuals: public works, federal installations, development grants, tax breaks, special immigration bills, and the like. Opportunities for doing things for constituents and supporters, for which members can then claim credit, are abundant and widely exploited.[5]

The further subdivision of committees into subcommittees also provides opportunities for claiming credit. "Whatever else it may be, the quest for specialization in Congress is a quest for credit. Every member can aspire to occupy a part of at least one piece of policy turf small enough so that he can claim personal responsibility for some of the things that happen on it." [6] Writing in the early 1970s, Mayhew observed that "the House may have to create more subcommittees to satisfy its members." [7] That is exactly what it did; the number of standing subcommittees grew from 120 to 151 between 1971 and 1975.

The creation of more subcommittees was only one of many changes in House organization made in the early 1970s. These changes added up to a major transformation in the way Congress does its business. Although they had varied sources, among the most important were developments in the electoral politics of Congress. One essential factor was the influx of a large number

[5] William J. Crotty and Gary C. Jacobson, *American Parties in Decline* (Boston: Little, Brown, 1980), pp. 202–203.

[6] Mayhew, *Electoral Connection*, pp. 85–94.

[7] Ibid., p. 95.

of new members who won office as energetic purveyors of the kind of entrepreneurial politics described in this book.

High incumbent reelection rates have not prevented a large turnover in House membership. Quite the opposite. The principle reason is that voluntary retirements were much more common in the 1970s than in the previous two decades. From 1946 through 1970, the average number of voluntary retirements from the House was twenty-eight; from 1972 through 1980, it was forty-one. The average number of Senate retirements was five in the earlier period, seven in the later.[8] Among the many reasons for this change are the heavier demands of entrepreneurial electoral politics. Constant cultivation of the district provides the margin of electoral safety; but it is an endless, time-consuming chore. The personal cost of holding onto the individual political franchise has gone up; for more than a few, it eventually becomes too high. One House member who gave up a safe seat, Otis Pike of New York, put it this way:

> Being expected to put in a full day's work at the office and a full night's appearance on the banquet circuit can get to be and has come to be a bore. . . . People bug me more than they used to. They are asking their government to do more for them and are willing to do less and less for themselves. . . . So much of the work is nit-picking trivia.[9]

The other major source of new members was the 1974 election, which put seventy-eight freshman Democrats into the House.

The new members tended to be markedly different from their elders. In particular, they were more adept at, and more comfortable with, the new styles of electoral politics. This was especially true of Democrats who had replaced Republicans. Their precarious electoral position inspired imaginative cultivation of constituencies and aggressively independent behavior in Wash-

---

[8] Calculated from data in John F. Bibby, Thomas E. Mann, and Norman J. Ornstein, *Vital Statistics on Congress, 1980* (Washington, D.C.: American Enterprise Institute for Public Policy Research, 1980), pp. 14–15.

[9] Joseph Cooper and William West, "The Congressional Career in the 1970s," in *Congress Reconsidered,* 2nd ed., eds. Lawrence C. Dodd and Bruce I. Oppenheimer (Washington, D.C.: Congressional Quarterly Press, 1981), p. 90.

ington.[10] All the new members entered Congress at a time when party coalitions were dissolving and party organizations were moribund in many places. Most of them had come of political age during a decade of assassination, violent protest, the Vietnam War, environmental alarms, energy shortages, political scandal, and a decline in respect for authority of all kinds, but especially that of political institutions and leaders. Like other Americans of their generation, they were typically better educated, more independent of party, less awed by age and authority than were their predecessors. They shared the conviction that they were elected to lead, not follow.

People who win office under present conditions evidently feel they cannot afford to be patient. It is scarcely surprising that the new generation of congressmen refused to wait around docilely until time, electoral security, and the seniority system elevated them to positions of power in Congress. Instead, they helped alter the rules to assure themselves of a solid piece of legislative turf early in their careers. The large classes of new House Democrats provided the votes that effectively undermined the seniority system, disaggregated legislative authority from the committee to the subcommittee level, solidified the power of subcommittee chairmen, and distributed subcommittee chairmanships and seats on desirable subcommittees more widely. All of these changes were enacted over the protest of a majority of senior members, who naturally stood to lose much of the power and influence they had patiently accumulated playing by the old rules. Junior members have been their chief beneficiaries.[11]

As a consequence, authority in Congress is more fragmented than ever, making it more difficult to build coalitions, coordinate decisions, and make policy. These changes served the immediate needs of individual members, but at the price of eroding Congress's ability to make coherent national policy. The collective interests of congressmen were therefore threatened. The threat

[10] Charles M. Tidmarch, "The Second Time Around: Freshman Democratic House Members' 1976 Reelection Experiences" (Paper delivered during the Annual Meeting of the American Political Science Association, Washington, D.C., September 1–4, 1977); Crotty and Jacobson, *Parties in Decline,* pp. 196–201.

[11] Ibid., pp. 206–212.

did not go unnoticed, and it was met, significantly, by changes designed to strengthen the congressional party.

The Congressional Parties

The inherent tension between individual electoral pursuits and the behavior required for Congress to function effectively is brought into sharpest focus in the congressional parties. Parties are the primary institutional devices for organizing collective action. A decentralized and specialized legislative system could not work effectively without some means for coordinating the activities of its diverse parts. The fragmented activity must be reduced to some order, the diverse membership welded together from time to time into majority coalitions, if Congress is to share in governing. This is what the congressional parties are for. They work to counteract the centrifugal tendencies inherent in the committee system as well as in the electoral politics of Congress.[12]

Members of Congress recognize that the parties make a vital contribution to institutional achievement, and not a little of the deference accorded party leaders derives from this.[13] But the demands of electoral politics raise formidable barriers to party control. Congressional parties and their leaders do not control access to office; their ability to discipline members is therefore severely limited from the start. Furthermore, party leaders are quick to recognize electoral necessity; members are expected to "vote the district first" when conflicts with the party's position arise, and they are encouraged to serve their constituents well in order to keep the seat for the party. There is nothing odd about this, for the leaders are themselves chosen to serve their party's members as they wish to be served. Such permissiveness simply reflects a widely acknowledged necessity produced by the diversity of national party coalitions and current notions about how to win reelection.

The benefits of tolerant party leadership are apparent to congressmen, but so are the costs. Thus when the committee and

[12] Ibid., p. 203.
[13] Mayhew, *Electoral Connection,* pp. 145–149.

seniority systems were altered to serve the individual needs of members at the expense of Congress's ability to get anything useful accomplished, changes designed to strengthen the parties were also adopted. The speaker, who leads the majority party in the House, was given control of the Rules Committee (he appoints all of its members), which directs the flow of legislation coming to the floor of the House, and dominant influence on the Democratic Caucus' Steering and Policy Committee, which, among other things, makes committee assignments. He was also authorized to appoint ad hoc committees to handle specific pieces of legislation. This allows the Speaker to give bills to a committee whose members are chosen for their willingness to cooperate with him. Sensitive and controversial legislation like welfare reform, energy policy, and the House's own earnings limitation and financial disclosure measures were given to ad hoc committees in the 95th Congress.[14] The party's whip organization was also enlarged substantially. These changes have given the party leaders more tools to coordinate and combine the work of an increasingly fragmented body. Whether they are sufficient to offset other changes in rules, habits, and structures is another question.

There is nothing self-contradictory or unprecedented about changes that give members more independent authority and leaders more tools to manage congressional business. They simply reflect the conflicting needs and motives of congressmen. Party leaders perform the chores necessary to maintain institutional effectiveness and are rewarded with authority, influence, and deference. As structural and behavioral changes make their task more difficult, other changes are adopted that enhance their authority and influence.

The Budgetary Process

Party leaders are not the only members of Congress who are granted influence and deference for doing the institutionally essential dirty work. At the time Mayhew was writing, members of committees that raised and spent money were also given spe-

[14] Richard E. Cohen, "Tip O'Neill — He Gets By With a Little Help from His Friends," *National Journal* 10 (September 2, 1978):1386–1388.

cial status and various legislative privileges in return for saving Congress from the collective effects of its tolerant individualism. Appropriations guarded the treasury, preventing all the pork-barrelling and log-rolling from sending the national debt into orbit. Tax legislation coming out of Ways and Means was routinely granted a closed rule, forbidding amendments, to prevent a scramble for tax breaks that would sap revenues and remove any final shreds of integrity from the tax structure. Such committees were expected to protect Congress from itself and were given the authority to do so.[15]

These mechanisms of institutional self-control were eroded by the same forces that transformed the committee and party structures. Newer members of these committees shared neither the electoral security (thus freedom of maneuver) nor the penny-pinching ethos of traditional money committee members. New rules regarding seniority and subcommittee organization weakened committee leadership. The move toward more "openness," which was part of the newer style of operation, made it harder for individual members to agree collectively to forego pushing politically popular projects of dubious worth. Inhibitions against offering floor amendments to fiscal legislation diminished. Aggressively independent junior members, no longer inclined to defer to any institutional authority, became adept at finding ways to circumvent the normal budgetary process to put their favorite programs into action.[16]

More assertive political individualism, growing out of a changed electoral environment, sharpened the conflict between personal and collective congressional goals. Each member has a separate interest in providing programs that please supporters without worrying about the collective impact on the budget of all of them doing the same thing. But the aggregate result is too much spending. That means either raising taxes or having too large a deficit, neither politically desirable. The money committees (especially in the House) worked against this tendency with declining effect after the reforms had taken root.

[15] Mayhew, *Electoral Connection,* pp. 152–156.
[16] Allen Schick, "The Three-Ring Budget Process: The Appropriations, Tax, and Budget Committees in Congress," in *The New Congress,* eds. Thomas E. Mann and Norman J. Ornstein (Washington, D.C.: American Enterprise Institute, 1981), pp. 297–304.

The problem was all the more serious because an important external constraint on congressional largesse stopped working properly at about the same time. By the early 1970s, Congress had come to rely on the president to save it (and the country) from the aggregate consequences of excessive individual generosity. If no one in Congress paid other than symbolic heed to the fiscal effects of the balance of expenditures and revenues generated by the budget each year, the president certainly did. Presidents wisely concern themselves with such comprehensive fiscal questions, because the health of the economy is closely related to their political fortunes. The president, with congressional acquiescence, took to impounding — refusing to spend — some of the funds authorized and appropriated by Congress in order to keep spending totals from reaching unacceptable levels. Members could still claim credit for enacting programs, but they could avoid the embarrassment of having to present the bill for them to the public.

The Nixon presidency ended this comfortable arrangement. Nixon used impoundment to impose his own spending priorities on Congress and to subvert those of the Democratic majority rather than to protect Congress from its own folly. Even appropriations passed over his veto were impounded. This fundamental challenge to the institutional authority of Congress — the taxing and spending powers lie at the heart of it — did not go unanswered. The answer was the 1974 Congressional Budget and Impoundment Control Act. It put presidential impoundment authority under the strict scrutiny and control of Congress. More importantly, it set up internal structures and procedures to assure that impoundment would not be necessary to keep the gap between revenue and spending from becoming too wide.

A Budget Committee was established in each house. They were assigned the task of keeping congressional spending and revenue raising policies in harmony. Each spring, the budget committees must report a budget resolution setting spending and revenue targets for the fiscal year beginning the following October. Once the budget resolution is adopted, the regular committees go to work on their segments of the budget as before. But now they are expected to abide by the limits imposed by the budget resolution. In the fall, when work on the appropriations and tax bills has finished, the budget committees review the results. If the targets set in the spring have not been met, the budget committees can recommend reducing spending, raising taxes, or revising original goals for the size of the deficit (or, at least in theory, surplus). Congress is thus forced to choose explicitly how large a deficit we will have. It must acknowledge the fiscal consequences of the myriad separate decisions that are made during the session.

The new budget process is an excellent example of how electoral politics affect the internal structure of Congress. The fragmented pursuit of reelection threatens Congress's ability to govern itself and the nation; institutional structures are established to cope with the threat; when they fail, new mechanisms of self-control are erected. There is no reason to expect them to work perfectly. They do not; contrary impulses are always at work. Members quickly learned to use the new system to appear generous and tight-fisted at the same time. "That's the beauty of the budget process," explained one House member. "You can vote for all your favorite programs, and then vote against the deficit." [17] But it does put members on the spot individually as they make collective fiscal choices. Ironically, in light of its genesis, the new process has also made it easier for the president to impose his own budget policies, at least under certain conditions. (The subject of presidential leadership is explored more fully later.)

Particularism

Electoral politics affects congressional policy making through its impact on rules and structures, but this does not exhaust its influence. The entire system of congressional politics is permeated by considerations of electoral necessity. They establish patterns of congressional concern and responsiveness and have a profound effect on who wins and who loses in the competition for favorable government decisions. The most obvious example is the traditional interest members have shown in policies that produce particularized benefits.[18] Legislation which provides specific tangible projects that produce most or all of

[17] Joel Havemann, "Budget Process Nearly Ambushed by Carter and by Congress," *National Journal* 9 (May 21, 1977):787.
[18] Mayhew, *Electoral Connection,* pp. 53–54 and passim.

their benefits for individual states or districts — water projects are familiar examples — has typically excited the most congressional interest. It is no coincidence that Congress has fought hard to maintain control over decisions allocating such projects or that universalistic distributive criteria are used in selecting them — every district gets a share.[19] It is an article of firm belief among members of Congress that credit claimed for federally funded local projects pays important electoral dividends.

But the concern with particularized benefits goes beyond public works. Virtually any proposal will attract more support if the benefits it is designed to provide can be chopped up and allocated in identifiable packages to individual states and districts. Since everyone in Washington knows this, policies are deliberately designed to distribute particularized benefits broadly even when this makes no objective sense. If the original proponents of a program do not make the necessary · adjustments, Congress will do it for them. Douglas Arnold, who has many useful things to say about these matters, offers some examples:

> The idea behind model cities was to create a demonstration program pouring massive federal funds into a handful of troubled cities. Congress transformed it completely by providing for 150 cities, making small cities eligible, and limiting any state's share to 15 percent of the total funds. Bureaucrats then selected the cities strategically, for maximum political effect, spreading the benefits among as many of the program's congressional supporters as possible, even selecting a handful of villages with populations under 5,000. Similarly, a water and sewer program (1965) conceived to help rapidly growing areas was transformed so that all areas were eligible. The Appalachian regional development programs (and most other economic development programs) have been broadened to include less distressed areas. The poverty program (1964), conceived as an experiment that would concentrate funds in pockets of poverty, evolved into a program with benefits spread thinly across the country. The list could go on.[20]

[19] Carter got off to a bad start with Congress by vetoing a public works bill. On universalistic criteria, see Mayhew, *Electoral Connection*, pp. 88–89.

[20] R. Douglas Arnold, "The Local Roots of Domestic Policy," in *The New Congress*, eds. Thomas E. Mann and Norman J. Ornstein (Washington, D.C.: American Enterprise Institute for Public Policy Research, 1981), p. 272. This and following Arnold material reprinted by permission.

The consequences are clear from these examples. Often resources are not concentrated where they are needed most (or where they can be used most efficiently by any objective criterion). They are wasted and their impact is diluted. Grandly conceived programs emerge in a form that often ensures that they will fail to achieve their objectives, feeding doubts that the federal government can do anything effectively.

Arnold identifies similar problems in the formulas that allocate funds under categorical grant programs. After studying the 140 or so formulas now in use, his "most striking discovery is how infrequently formulas are constructed around merit criteria." [21] Programs

> ignore legitimate differences in demand. The program whose purpose it is to make railroad crossings safer hands out funds under a formula that counts population, area, and postal-route mileage, but not railroad crossings. Law enforcement grants reflect population, not the incidence of crime. Hunter safety grants ignore the concentration of hunters in rural areas. Urban mass transit grants reflect urban population and density, but not how many people actually use mass transit. New York, a city built around mass transit, receives a subsidy of two cents per transit passenger, while Grand Rapids, a product of the automobile, reaps forty-five cents per passenger.[22]

The search for equitable formulas follows a consistent path. The House prefers formulas using criteria of population; the Senate views things from the perspective of equality among states. The compromise solution is to use the population criterion, but with a minimum and maximum allocation for each state. "The ceilings usually affect only the largest two or three states and thus do little to diminish House majorities. The floors, which benefit perhaps a dozen small states, contribute generously to Senate majorities. These simple maneuvers, though difficult to defend on policy grounds, consistently yield large, stable majorities." [23]

As a final irony, Arnold explains how the new computer technology has exacerbated the problem. Members can now calcu-

---

[21] Ibid., p. 268.
[22] Ibid.
[23] Ibid., p. 270.

late to a nicety the share their state or district is likely to receive from any variation in a distribution formula. Local interests, being sharply defined, must be defended (potential opponents find ready ammunition if they are not), so the pursuit of both agreement and efficiency is hindered.[24]

Serving the Organized

Another important consequence of electoral politics is that Congress serves the vocal and organized.[25] The system naturally favors any politically attentive group that is present in significant numbers in a large number of states or districts. The best examples are veterans (widely distributed, well organized) and social security recipients (widely distributed, large numbers, consistent voters). The way the Reagan administration's budget-cutting juggernaut was stopped dead when it took on social security is instructive. Congress, on its side, has shown no stomach at all for taking any steps to shore up the integrity of the system because all likely efforts would involve either cutting benefits or raising payroll taxes substantially.

Large numbers are not, however, essential for groups to be influential. Organization and money also matter. It is easy to exaggerate the threat that political action committees pose to democracy,[26] but their electoral importance has clearly been growing and it would be surprising if their political clout had not been keeping pace. They need not "buy" members with their contributions to be effective. Some of the most successful groups — the National Rifle Association (vigorous opponents of gun control legislation) and anti-abortionists are examples — win by the implicit threat to finance and work for the opponents of members who do not support their positions. A few instances where such groups have helped to defeat seemingly entrenched incumbents are sufficient to keep most members from taking them on. The NRA was widely credited with defeating gun con-

24 Ibid., p. 285–286.
25 Mayhew, *Electoral Connection*, pp. 130–131.
26 Michael J. Malbin, "Of Mountains and Molehills: PACs, Campaigns, and Public Policy," in *Parties, Interest Groups, and Campaign Finance Laws*, ed. Michael J. Malbin (Washington, D.C.: American Enterprise Institute for Public Policy Research, 1980), pp. 152–210.

trol proponent Senator Joseph Tydings of Maryland in 1970 and has been regarded as a major electoral force ever since. Iowa Senator Dick Clark's defeat in 1978 was attributed to the work of anti-abortion "Right to Life" activists who were, of course, delighted to take credit for it.

The prospect of being targeted by any group with formidable campaign resources is unsettling; most members prefer to keep a low profile, avoiding votes that consistently offend active, well-organized groups. At one time, for example, Environmental Action, a conservation lobbying group, compiled and publicized a list of the "Dirty Dozen," twelve congressmen who had (by Environmental Action's standards) bad records on environmental issues and who seemed vulnerable. Over five elections, twenty-four of the fifty-two who made the Dirty Dozen list were defeated. Peter Harnick, a consultant who worked on the campaigns, claimed that the tactic "was very effective at making congressmen think twice about certain votes. There were numerous examples of members or their staff calling and saying 'Is the congressman close to being on the list?' or 'Is this vote going to be used to determine the list?' " [27]

Keeping a low profile has become more difficult in recent years. Reforms intended to open congressional activities to greater public scrutiny have worked; the action is more visible now, with more public meetings and more recorded votes. Members are thereby exposed to more pressure from interest and constituency groups. Lobbyists have been quick to take advantage; there was a notable increase in the sophistication and effectiveness of Washington lobbyists in the 1970s. In the 95th Congress (1977–1979), for instance,

> business organizations, taking their cue from public affairs activists such as Common Cause and Ralph Nader, organized highly effective grass roots lobbying campaigns and were able, for example, to block enactment of legislation establishing a consumer protection agency.
>
> The anti-abortion lobby was responsible for the enactment of strict language prohibiting the government from paying for most abortions with Medicaid funds or military appropriations.

[27] "The Trail of the 'Dirty Dozen,' " *C.Q. Weekly Report* 39 (March 21, 1981):510.

The Women's lobby was surprisingly successful in persuading Congress to extend for thirty-nine months the deadline for ratification of the Equal Rights Amendment.

The Health industry took on the administration on the question of mandatory ceilings on hospital rates and prevented one of the president's most significant bills from being enacted.[28]

Shrewd interest groups have learned to combine their work in Washington with work at the grass roots. The trick is to organize a stream of messages from the district that, at the very least, encourage members to listen attentively to the pitch made by the group's Washington spokesmen. Party leaders and the president's political advisors have discovered this strategy as well, of which more later.

All of these developments have limited members' political maneuverability. Much of what they do is now visible to too many groups with too much capacity to bring them electoral trouble for the politics of accommodation and compromise to work as easily as it once did. Building coalitions in the face of widespread conflict and disagreement is a more difficult task than ever because it is so much harder to make political deals when they must be "open covenants openly arrived at." The task of party or presidential leadership, of making coherent national policy, is clearly more arduous. Congress's capacity to govern is thereby diminished. If Congress cannot deal with serious national problems, power will flow to those political institutions that can.

Immobility

Congress has been known for years to be an exceptionally deliberate deliberative body. As Nelson Polsby once suggested, Congress is not "designed to be fast on its 1070 feet." [29] Its mode of operation, rooted in the system of electoral politics by which its members are chosen, obviously encourages delay and usually frustrates anyone seeking quick and decisive action. But Fenno

---

[28] *C.Q. Weekly Report* 36 (October 21, 1978):3000.

[29] Nelson W. Polsby, *Congress and the Presidency,* 3rd ed. (Englewood Cliffs, New Jersey: Prentice-Hall, 1976), p. 16.

points out that this is not always a bad thing. His persuasive example is the process by which Richard Nixon was forced from office. Lengthy hearings, first by the Ervin Committee in the Senate, then by the House Judiciary Committee considering articles of impeachment, worked slowly but surely to build up a consensus among both political elites and the mass public that Nixon had indeed violated the law (not to mention basic rules of the political game) and should go. What might have been a traumatic source of sharp political conflict — the resignation of a sitting president for the first time in history — was, in the end, greeted with widespread approval and relief. The process as well as the evidence it publicized was essential to making Nixon's expulsion from public life legitimate.[30]

What is a virtue under some conditions is a defect under others. And there is a distinction between a slow process that builds to consensus and the kind of immobility displayed by Congress in recent years in the face of serious national problems (energy policy is the most notorious example). At present, though, it appears that (1) it is harder than ever to build policy coalitions in Congress, and (2) we face more pressing national problems that cannot be resolved by resort to the particularistic distributive criteria favored by congressional processes. I return to this point later in the chapter.

Even under more favorable conditions, Congress is weakened by the basic problem that the work members must do to make the institution strong pays few electoral dividends. Hard legislative work is largely invisible to the folks back home. A successful legislative career is no guarantee of electoral success. The powerful senior House Democrats who were defeated in 1980 attest to that. Members' resources of time and energy, even staff, are limited; the time spent on legislative work cannot be spent shoring up constituency support. The results of 1980 raise the possibility that the more powerful and effective members become in Washington and the greater their contribution to institutional performance, the more vulnerable they are to challengers. This sharpens the dilemma for members who desire to

[30] Richard F. Fenno, Jr., *Home Style: House Members in Their Districts* (Boston: Little, Brown, 1978), p. 245.

be reelected but who recognize that election is not an end in itself, only a means to a share in governing the nation. The danger is that perhaps the more one participates in governing, the more one is likely to be defeated. That its members face such a dilemma must weaken Congress as an institution no matter how they resolve it.

Symbolism

The electoral politics of Congress also encourages activity that is heavy on symbolism and light on actual results. Members seek (and get) credit for taking the proper positions, making agreeable speeches, casting correct votes without these actions having any necessary connection to real policy decisions. Mayhew makes the point succinctly: "We can all point to a good many instances in which congressmen seem to have gotten into trouble by being on the *wrong* side in a roll call vote, but who can think of one where a member got into trouble by being on the *losing* side?" [31] Offering as an example a vote on a bill to stop busing, he notes that "congressmen had every reason to worry about whether they were voting on the right side but no reason to worry about what passed or was implemented." [32] They are held responsible for taking the right position, not for being successful. Again, it is obvious where the incentives lie. Making good public policy is rewarded no better than just talking about it, and it consumes a good deal more time, energy, and staff resources.

Building Coalitions

Building and sustaining policy coalitions, rarely easy given the realities of American political life, has become an even more formidable challenge in recent years. A more fragmented system of electoral politics begets more fragmented congressional politics. Barbara Sinclair, who examined congressional voting patterns on fifty-one key roll call votes taken in seven issue areas in the 95th Congress, found that, among Democrats in both houses,

[31] Mayhew, *Electoral Connection,* p. 117.
[32] Ibid., p. 115.

... coalitions were quite fluid; few Democrats were highly reliable across all issue areas; few could be written off. As a result, coalition building was more complex. The number of members the leadership had to contact and persuade had grown. Gauging the probability of winning was more difficult, and so was deciding how to spend scarce time and resources.[33]

Democrats had been divided in the past, of course, but the divisions were predictably sectional, distinguishing southerners from the rest. Sectional divisions remain, but in a changed form, with new cleavages superimposed over them. Republicans remain somewhat less divided, although members from the northeast are much more likely to bolt the party on every kind of issue.

Generational cleavages are apparent in both parties on policy as well as on procedural matters. Northern freshman and sophomore Democrats in the 95th Congress were significantly less supportive of the Democrats' traditional ally, organized labor, for example. Ironically, these newer Democratic members received much more campaign money from labor groups than did their seniors (who were less in need of it). But votes are more important than money. Their reluctance to support labor's proposals was directly connected to their electoral circumstances. Almost half of them had been elected to seats that had previously been held by Republicans, and it is this subgroup that diverged most strikingly from older Democrats on labor-related issues.[34] More generally, Sinclair found monotonically decreasing levels of party support among northern House Democrats the more recent their first election; the most unreliable members were those who replaced Republicans.[35]

Younger House Republicans also differ from their elders; they are more rigid ideologically and less likely to cooperate with the Democrats to make policy. As a result, party unity among House Republicans increased slightly in the late 1970s (presaging the strongly unified stance taken by Republicans on Reagan's

[33] Barbara Sinclair, "Coping with Uncertainty: Building Coalitions in the House and Senate," *The New Congress*, p. 215.

[34] William Schneider and Gregory Schell, "The New Democrats," *Public Opinion* 1 (November/December, 1978):7–13.

[35] Sinclair, "Building Coalitions," pp. 205–206.

budget and tax proposals in 1981). This meant more headaches for Democratic leaders, who could count on fewer votes from the other side of the aisle for their policy coalitions.[36]

The Issues

The greater fluidity of coalitions and difficulty of constructing them cannot be blamed entirely on changes in electoral styles and institutional processes. At least as important are closely related changes in the kinds of issues Congress is expected to resolve. The federal government has, in recent years, faced a host of tough decisions that directly affect how millions of people live. The problems and solutions divide the traditional party coalitions. Energy policy is an example: it splits Congress by region and state. Oil and gas producing states have interests directly contrary to those of energy consuming states. On this and other economic issues, states of the "snow belt," the northeast and the midwest, oppose states of the "sun belt," the south, southwest, and west. Formal groups have even been established in Congress to protect regional interests. Environmental policy is another example. It divides college-educated, middle-class Democrats from labor-oriented Democrats who would give priority to economic growth. It is a problem for Republicans, too, as they try to woo young, upwardly-mobile independents while supporting business demands for less regulation and more freedom to develop land and other natural resources. Social issues — abortion, school prayers, women's rights, affirmative action — produce another set of divisions across constituencies and parties and thus in Congress. The list could go on; the crucial point is that these issues divide people, states, districts, and thus members of Congress in different ways. Coherent and consistent battle lines are absent, so it is little wonder that coalitions tend to be ad hoc and fluid.

An even greater problem is the change in the nature of issues that have reached the agenda. Congress's electoral and institutional activities combine most harmoniously when politics can focus on distributing benefits. In periods of prosperity and growth, public and private resources expand together, and Con-

36 Ibid., pp. 207–208.

gress can busy itself with the happy chore of figuring out how to divide up a growing pie. Universalistic distributive criteria — something for everyone — are applicable and log-rolling coalitions relatively easy to assemble. The 1960s were just such a period.

The past decade, however, has been one of slower growth, higher inflation, and higher taxes needed to pay for the benefits so generously provided when the economy was booming. Instead of the pleasant prospect of distributing benefits, Congress increasingly faces the dismal task of distributing costs. Any of the proposed solutions to fundamental economic and social problems require that costs be imposed on some groups. If we have not actually become what Lester Thurow calls a "Zero-Sum Society," in which a gain by any group necessitates an equal loss by some other group,[37] it is certainly true that *redistribution* of limited resources is a more pressing issue than it used to be.

Congress is particularly ill-adapted to deal with redistributive questions. The system of electoral and complementary congressional politics that has evolved in recent years renders it painfully difficult to impose costs on any politically significant group. Most are too alert and too well organized, the policy process is too transparent, and members of Congress are too sensitive to too many demands. It is too easy to figure out who it will cost how much to carry out any policy and too easy to block any decision that threatens some loss.

Presidential Leadership

Such was plainly the lesson of the Carter administration, which had an extraordinarily difficult time getting what it wanted from a Congress that was, after all, controlled by Democrats. An exasperated Stuart Eizenstat (Carter's domestic policy chief) complained that "Moses would have difficulty getting the Ten Commandments through [Congress] today."[38] But the Reagan administration was surprisingly successful in getting Congress to enact its budget and tax programs in the first half

[37] Lester Thurow, *The Zero-Sum Society: Distribution and the Possibilities for Economic Change* (Harmondsworth, England: Penguin Books, 1981).

[38] Quoted in Sinclair, "Building Coalitions," p. 178.

of 1981. Why was Reagan so much more persuasive than Carter? Put another way, how can the president lead the contemporary Congress?

Political savvy helps. Part of the explanation is surely that the Reagan administration is simply more astute, politically, in its dealings with the Congress. Near the end of his second year in office, Carter revealed the breathtaking naivete that permeated his early efforts to get his programs through Congress. "We had an overly optimistic impression that I could present a bill to Congress which seemed to me patently in the best interest of our country and that the Congress would take it and pretty well pass it. I have been disabused of that expectation." [39] Presidents naturally view things from a national perspective; they are held responsible, by the electorate as well as history, for the national consequences of federal policies and programs. Congressional fates are decided locally, however, and so members are necessarily attentive to local interests. Those who are not are replaced by those who are. Anyone with a grasp of national politics knows this. Nor is how to persuade members of Congress to support a president's programs a great mystery: convince them that their own local electoral interests are served by cooperating with the president. Carter never learned to do this effectively; Reagan clearly knew the value of doing it from the start.

One strategy is to support members' local projects and pet programs in return for support for what the administration wants. "Washington is very much a city of 'You scratch my back, I'll scratch your back,'" observed Representative Norman Mineta in 1978. But Carter, he said, dealt "with issues on a vertical plane. He won't say to you "I need your vote on Mideast arms sales and therefore I will give you the dam you want in your district." [40] Reagan has no such scruples, as his reported effort to get the Senate to allow the sale of the AWACS reconnaissance planes to Saudi attests.[41] Even his budget and tax measures contained compromises that granted concessions to members, many

[39] Quoted in Joel Havemann, "Will Late-Session Success Spoil Jimmy Carter?" *National Journal* 10 (December 2, 1978):1943.

[40] Quoted in *C.Q. Weekly Report* 36 (September 2, 1978):2304.

[41] "Reagan Team May Draw Key Lessons from Difficult Struggle Over AWACS," *C.Q. Weekly Report* 39 (October 31, 1981):2098–2099.

of them Democrats, whose votes were considered crucial.[42]

Cutting the budget of course eliminated many programs and projects that are the basic currency of electoral politics. Costs were imposed disproportionately on some groups; Reagan's economic policies were intended to redistribute income from poorer to wealthier groups, at least in the short run. One reason many in Congress could be persuaded to cut social welfare programs is that the victims of the cuts are among those least likely to vote; they are largely unorganized and have few other political resources. But a more important reason was the perception that Reagan and his program were popular.

The president's level of popular support is a major source of variation in his influence with Congress. The traditional wisdom was articulated by a member of the Carter administration involved in congressional liaison in this manner: "When you go up to the Hill and the latest polls show Carter isn't doing well, there isn't much reason for a member to go along with him. There's little we can do if the member is not persuaded on the issue." [43] Carter did not enjoy broad public support during most of his presidency. Like other presidents, he was most popular early in his term — indeed, his early approval ratings were as high or higher than Reagan's — but he was unable to turn public support into political influence. A major problem was that he had overloaded his agenda with complicated and controversial legislation. Reagan was much more careful to exploit his early-term public support — plus the increment of esteem and affection that followed an attempt on his life — to bend Congress to his will. His administration's energies were concentrated on one major piece of legislation at a time, and much was made of the "mandate" he had supposedly received from voters to carry out his campaign promises to cut taxes and domestic spending while increasing the military budget. The shift of the Senate to Republican control made the claim of a mandate more credible and also, of course, made it much easier for the Republican administration to have its way.

---

[42] "White House's Lobbying Apparatus Produces Impressive Tax Vote Victory," *C.Q. Weekly Report* 39 (August 1, 1981):1372–1373.

[43] Quoted in *C.Q. Weekly Report* 36 (March 4, 1978):586.

The reasoning followed by members of Congress is straight-forward. If constituents like and support the president, then at least some of them will reward or punish their representatives according to how loyally they support the president's programs. Local activists, campaign contributors, and potential primary and general election opponents will consider support in their strategic calculations. Close association with a popular president will help discourage serious opposition. Conversely, separating oneself from an unpopular president of one's own party may also be a very wise move, as many Republicans learned to their dismay in 1974. Nixon's staunchest supporters suffered the consequences at the polls.[44]

Reagan reportedly won some Democratic votes for his pro-grams by promising not to campaign personally against Demo-crats in the House who were consistent supporters of his pro-posals.[45] Actually, there is no evidence that presidents really help their party's candidates by stumping for them at the midterm, but as long as members of Congress think they might (remem-ber the problem of uncertainty) the possibility remains a use-ful source of political influence. Perhaps more important is the implicit suggestion that no serious challenge in any form will be mounted against cooperative members of the opposing party. In any case, the empirical evidence does indicate that popular presidents have more success in their dealings with Congress than unpopular ones.[46]

The Reagan administration also took pains to make sure that the general perception of Reagan's popularity was given specific district focus. This work shows a canny understanding of how to influence Congress most effectively under current conditions. The administration stimulated an avalanche of messages — let-ters, telegrams, telephone calls — from the districts of House members who were considered persuadable to the president's

---

[44] See Gerald C. Wright, Jr., "Constituency Response to Congressional Behavior: The Impact of the House Judiciary Committee Impeachment Votes," *Western Political Quarterly* 30 (1977):401–410.

[45] "Conservative Southerners Are Enjoying Their Wooing as Key to Tax Bill Success," *C.Q. Weekly Report* 39 (June 13, 1981):1025.

[46] Douglas Rivers and Nancy L. Rose, "Passing the President's Program: Public Opinion and Presidential Influence in Congress" (Prepared for de-livery at the 1981 Annual Meeting of the Midwestern Political Science Association, Cincinnati, Ohio, April 16–18, 1981).

side in the budget battles. Democratic Representative Dan Glickman of Kansas, for example, reported receiving 1,500 phone calls urging him to support Reagan's tax bill. The technique of grassroots lobbying was convincing in a way that appeals to party loyalty or the national interest would never be.[47] Clearly, this is the most effective way to influence the current crop of congressmen. An administration that can maintain a political organization capable of mobilizing grassroots sentiment after the election is certain to be more successful in its dealings with Congress.

Democratic Speaker Thomas P. "Tip" O'Neill, the public victim of Reagan's triumphs, made a similar discovery during the Carter administration. O'Neill was, in fact, remarkably successful in pushing Carter's programs, given the odds he faced. One reason for this was that he developed unobtrusive methods of party influence. Rather than make direct appeals for party loyalty, the Democratic leadership worked through influential groups in the districts of targeted members (mainly labor unions that had helped finance and conduct their campaigns). Stimulated by the party, these groups then worked to persuade the member to the party's position. Often the member did not suspect party influence at all.[48]

An additional factor in the Reagan administration's success was its clever exploitation of the budget process that Congress had, ironically, set up to strengthen itself against encroachments by the executive. The new process compels members to cast a few highly visible votes on the whole budget package. This provides a focal point where the president's persuasive efforts can be efficiently concentrated. Under the old system, which handled budgetary matters in a completely piecemeal fashion, even a popular president enjoying broad public support for his programs would find it difficult to bring pressure to bear on the many separate decisions that determined the aggregate fiscal product. The connection between any individual program or vote and the aggregate total was relatively easy to obscure. The

---

[47] "Tax Vote Victory," *C.Q. Weekly Report* 39 (August 1, 1981):1372.
[48] Lawrence Dodd and Terry Sullivan, "House Leadership Success in the Vote Gathering Process: A Comparative Analysis" (Paper delivered during the Annual Meeting of the Midwest Political Science Association, Chicago, April 24–26, 1980).

means Congress has chosen to control itself fiscally strengthens the hand of a president who commands widespread public support.

The Congress, as it now operates, *can* be led. At different times, both Tip O'Neill and Ronald Reagan have shown this to be true. The most effective techniques of persuasion are those which are adapted to the realities of electoral politics. But, Reagan's early successes notwithstanding, even the cleverest leadership is no guarantor of success. Conditions have to be just right; often they are not. Widespread, active public support for policies often cannot be generated. The Reagan administration relied on crisis rhetoric (hemorrhaging budgets requiring emergency surgery if the national patient were not to expire), the early term honeymoon, and Reagan's survival of an assassination attempt to push as hard and as quickly as possible to enact its spending and taxing packages. But it is hard to sustain a sense of crisis; popularity tends to decline over a president's term in office. A second attempt to slash the budget further as economic conditions worsened in the fall of 1981 fell flat; efforts to raise the alarm once again were half-hearted and ineffective. Reagan was threatened with the defection of House Republicans from the northeast who had gone along with the original cuts with some trepidation and, looking to the 1982 elections, were not willing to countenance changes that would take any more away from their constituents.

Other presidential initiatives were also roughly handled. The sale of AWACS to Saudi Arabia was strongly opposed by Senators of both parties and only squeaked through after a costly and frantic campaign featuring the argument that stopping the sale would severely damage the president's capacity to deal with foreign nations. Reagan's decision on a new land-based missile system was roundly attacked by the Republican right as well as by the Democratic left and not a few moderates. The point is that winning coalitions can be built in Congress, but they are inevitably shaky. Loyalty to party or the president cannot consistently overcome members' healthy concern with their own electoral fates. A congressional liaison official from the State Department put it this way: "It used to be that a central piece of information on a vote was the president's position. With the breakdown of party discipline, it is clear that voters expect members to exercise independent judgment. That means voting on the issue, not just to agree with the president." [49]

The developments I have traced here in congressional election politics make presidential leadership more difficult and, at the same time, more essential. Despite the dangers, all too familiar from the Johnson and Nixon administrations, of an Imperial Presidency, we must depend on the White House for national leadership, since the Congress is, by disposition and structure, incapable of providing it. Only the president — if anyone — is consistently motivated to consider general rather than particular needs, interests, and policy results. Only the president — if anyone — can find political advantage in policies that impose specific immediate costs on identifiable groups in the interest of greater general benefits in the future. Only the president has a continuing incentive to produce policies that are successful as well as symbolically satisfying, for only the president is held fully responsible by voters for the performance of the federal government. Electoral politics gives us a Congress that is responsive, but not responsible, a point that is elaborated in the next, and final, chapter.

[49] Quoted in *C.Q. Weekly Report* 36 (March 4, 1978):596.

8

Representation, Responsibility, and the Future of Congressional Elections

Congress is a representative assembly. Put most simply,[1] it is a representative assembly because its members are chosen in competitive popular elections, and if voters do not like what they are doing, they can vote them out of office. Voters can hold congressmen accountable for their actions as long as members care about reelection. Nearly everyone does. Representation is an effect of electoral politics; the electoral system structures the kind of representation Congress provides. What kind of representation is that?

Representation

Political scientists have customarily paid the most attention to one aspect of representation: policy congruence. The central question is the extent to which the policy views of people in a

---

[1] It is a complicated concept. See Hannah Pitkin, *The Concept of Representation* (Berkeley: University of California Press, 1967).

state or district are reflected in the policy stances (usually measured by roll-call votes) of the people they elect to Congress. This has never been an easy question to answer. Information on constituency opinion is scarce and often unreliable, and it is frequently doubtful that there is any "constituency opinion" on a given issue. Measuring constituency attitudes has challenged the ingenuity of a generation of scholars, since the one unquestioned solution — adequate sample surveys of a large number of states and districts — is simply too expensive.

Demographic indicators, simulations, referenda voting, and aggregated national survey data have all been used to estimate state and district attitudes.[2] Each of these approaches has its drawbacks, and there is the additional problem of establishing some kind of comparability between any of these measures and measures of congressional behavior.[3] Still, a number of general conclusions can be drawn from this work. Most research suggests that congressional roll-call votes are indeed related to estimated district opinion, although the strength of the connection varies across issue dimensions and is never overwhelmingly large. The relationships are strongest when votes and attitudes are combined and reduced to a few general dimensions — for example, domestic welfare policy or civil rights for minorities — and weaker for specific votes on single pieces of legislation.[4] The connection is also stronger if the constituency is defined as the member's supporters (defined by voting or partisanship).[5]

All of these findings make sense. Members of Congress develop highly differentiated images of their constituencies and have a fair notion of who keeps them in office. It is no surprise that they are more responsive to some groups than to others. There is not a great deal of pressure to vote district (or supporting constituency) preferences on every vote, especially since on many specific votes constituency preferences are unknown or

[2] For an account of this literature, see Walter J. Stone, "Measuring Constituency-Representative Linkages: Problems and Prospects," *Legislative Studies Quarterly* 4 (1979):624.

[3] Ibid., pp. 624–626.

[4] Compare Stone, "Linkages," with Gillian Dean, John Siegfried, and Leslie Ward, "Constituency Preference and Potential Economic Gain: Cues for Senate Voting on the Family Assistance Plan," *American Politics Quarterly* 9 (1981):341–356.

[5] Stone, "Linkages," pp. 632–634.

unformed. Members need only take care to cast "explainable" votes. On the other hand, anyone who consistently votes contrary to the wishes of his or her constituents is likely to run into trouble; a string of bad votes will attract serious opponents and give them ammunition.

Congress is broadly representative on another dimension. As we saw in Chapter 6, aggregate election results are responsive to national political and economic conditions. When things are going badly, the administration's party suffers the consequences. The opposing party picks up more seats, and even those who remain in Congress get the message that they had better watch their step. Reagan was able to win budget victories not only because more Republicans sit in the 97th Congress, but also because the remaining Democrats read the election results as a demand that something drastic be done about taxes and inflation. The issue in 1980 was not whether the budget and taxes would be cut, but which package of cuts — the administration's or the House Democrats' — would be adopted.

Aggregate representation of this kind is necessarily crude and rests on somewhat shaky foundations, depending, as it now does, on the self-reinforcing prophecies of congressional elites. And it can only operate when there is some public consensus on the general direction of policy. The energy crisis, designated by Carter as the "moral equivalent of war," was certainly the dominant national issue when gas lines developed and energy prices skyrocketed. But Congress could not produce any systematic plan to cope with it because all of the proposed solutions would impose major costs on politically powerful groups.

The scholarly interest in measuring degrees of policy congruence to assess congressional representation is in itself a consequence of congressional election politics. The question would scarcely arise in a system built around strong programmatic parties. If voters merely expressed a preference for a party's proposals in their vote and the winning party carried out its promised policies, policy representation would be automatic. Weak parties, the diversity of states and districts, pervasive electoral individualism, and the host of electoral activities that have nothing to do with national policy are what raise the issue in the first place. What kind of representation is provided by independent political entrepreneurs who stay in office by emphasizing constituent services and their own personal honesty, sincerity, and availability rather than policies or partisanship?

One of Fenno's important insights is that much of what goes on in the pursuit of congressional office is in fact essential to meaningful representation in a system without strong, programmatic parties.

> There is no way that the act of representing can be separated from the act of getting elected. If the congressman cannot win and hold the votes of some people, he cannot represent any people. Further, he cannot represent any people unless he knows, or makes an effort to know, who they are, what they think, and what they want; and it is by campaigning for electoral support among them that he finds out such things. During the expansionist stage of his constituency career, particularly, he probably knows his various constituencies as well as it is possible to know them. It is, indeed, by such campaigning, by going home a great deal, that a congressman develops a complex and discriminating set of perceptions about his constituents.[6]

This knowledge is the basis for making judgments about what constituents want or need from politics. Two-way communication is essential to representation. The stress members of Congress put on their accessibility invites communication from constituents at the same time it attracts their support. The knowledge and work it takes to win and hold a district not only establish the basis for policy congruence, but also let the member know when it is irrelevant or unnecessary.

There is much more to representation than policy congruence, of course. The work of Fenno and others has made that clear. Members certainly "represent" their constituents in important ways by helping them cope with the federal bureaucracy, by bringing in public works projects, by helping local governments and other groups to take advantage of federal programs, or by helping an overseas relative get permanent resident status. Particularized benefits are still benefits, and an important part of representation evidently involves making sure one's state or district gets its share.

[6] Richard F. Fenno, Jr., *Home Style: House Members in their Districts* (Boston: Little, Brown, 1978), p. 233.

Representation of still another kind is provided by members who take it on themselves to become spokesmen for interests and groups not confined to their constituencies. Black congressmen, for example, often present themselves as representatives of all Black Americans. Senator Jesse Helms takes it upon himself to represent the preferences of the ultraconservatives of the "New Right." Representative Henry Hyde leads the legislative fight against abortion and has become a major figure on the "Right-to-Life" speaking circuit. Opposition to the Vietnam War absorbed the energies of more than a few members some years back. Most members are not so careless that their commitment to a group or cause upsets their supporting constituency; more often it becomes a way of pleasing constituents (especially their core supporters) and so coincides nicely with electoral necessities. But not always. A few members invite consistently strong opposition and regularly court defeat in representing their vision of the national interest. The electoral system, however, tends to weed them out.

On a somewhat more mundane level, the current electoral process gives representation of a sort to any group that can mobilize people or money to help in campaigns. The corporate PACs, trade associations, labor unions, and ideological groups that provide campaign resources help to elect congenial candidates and gain, at least, access to them; both provide these groups with representation. It is a matter of debate whether this is a benign or pernicious phenomenon, and the controversy is not likely to die down as long as PAC contributions continue to grow. But it would be hard to argue that some mechanism for representing the enormous variety of economic and political interests that cannot be encompassed within the framework of single-member districts is not essential. With the decline of political parties, no obvious alternatives exist.

In one way Congress does not represent the American public well at all: demographically. It contains a much greater proportion of white, male, college-educated, professional, higher-income people than the population as a whole. Almost half of its present members are lawyers; a blue-collar background is rare. Yet it is probably quite representative of the kinds of people who achieve positions of leadership in the great majority of American institutions. It would be unlikely in the extreme for an electoral system like the American to produce a Congress looking anything like a random sample of the voting age population. What it does produce is a sample of local elites from an incredibly diverse, heterogeneous society. And from this perspective, a basic problem may be that the electoral politics of Congress generates legislative bodies that are *too* representative of the myriad divisions in American society.

American citizens are seriously divided themselves on most important political issues. But their divisions do not form coherent patterns. No clear political battle lines have developed across the range of contemporary issues. Most of the time there is little consensus on what issues are important, let alone what alternative solutions are preferable. Mayhew argues that "half the adverse criticism of Congress ... is an indirect criticism of the public itself." [7] Like the members of Congress whom they elect, Americans have wanted to have it both ways. We have enjoyed the programs and benefits that the federal government provides, but we dislike paying the price in the form of higher taxes, more inflation, and greater government regulation. Public opinion polls have found, in recent years, solid majorities for national health insurance, wage and price controls, government guarantees of jobs, and current or greater levels of spending on the environment, education, the cities, and health care. They have found equally solid majorities believing that the federal government is too large, spends too much money, and is too intrusive in peoples lives.[8] As Senator Lowell Weicker once put it, "everybody wants to go to Heaven, but nobody wants to die." [9]

Responsiveness without Responsibility

The dilemmas this creates for Congress reinforce the fundamental flaw in the kind of representation produced by electoral politics: great individual *responsiveness,* equally great collective *irresponsibility.* Emphasis on constituency services becomes

[7] David R. Mayhew, *Congress: The Electoral Connection* (New Haven: Yale University Press, 1974), p. 140.

[8] From a study by Everett C. Ladd, Jr., cited by George F. Will, "Slash 'Waste,' Cure Everything," *Hartford Courant,* December 14, 1978, p. 30.

[9] Quoted in William J. Crotty and Gary C. Jacobson, *American Parties in Decline* (Boston: Little, Brown, 1980), p. 242.

more attractive as policy matters become more divisive and threatening. Beyond that, the safest way to cope with contradictory policy demands is to be acutely sensitive to what constituent and other politically important groups want in taking positions but to avoid responsibility for the costs they would impose. Voting for all your favorite programs and then against the deficit total is the paradigmatic strategy. The pervasive temptation to engage in symbolic position taking rather than working to find real solutions to national problems is harder to resist when every solution is likely to anger one politically important group or another. It does not help matters that members are rewarded individually for taking pleasing positions but are not punished for failing to turn them into national policy or, when they do become policy, for seeing that they work.

As long as members are not held individually responsible for Congress' performance as an institution, a crucial form of representation is missing. Responsiveness is insufficient without responsibility. Political parties are the only instruments we have managed to develop for imposing collective responsibility on legislators. There is nothing original about this observation; it is a home truth to which students of congressional politics are inevitably drawn.[10] Morris Fiorina has recently put the case cogently:

> A strong political party can generate collective responsibility by creating incentives for leaders, followers, and popular supporters to think and act in collective terms. First, by providing party leaders with the capability (e.g., control of institutional patronage, nominations, etc.) to discipline party members, genuine leadership becomes possible. Legislative output is less likely to be a least common denominator — a residue of myriad conflicting proposals — and more likely to consist of a program actually intended to solve a problem or move the nation in a particular direction. Second, the subordination of individual officeholders to the party lessens their ability to separate themselves from party actions. Like it or not their performance becomes identified with the performance of the collectivity to which they belong. Third, with individual candidate variation greatly reduced,

[10] Mayhew, *Electoral Connection,* pp. 174–177; Morris P. Fiorina, "The Decline of Collective Responsibility in American Politics," *Daedalus* 109 (Summer, 1980):25–45.

voters have less incentive to support individuals and more to support or oppose the party as a whole. And fourth, the circle closes as party line voting in the electorate provides party leaders with the incentive to propose policies which will earn the support of a national majority, and party backbenchers with the personal incentive to cooperate with leaders in the attempt to compile a good record for the party as a whole.[11]

Pristine party government has never been characteristic of American politics, to be sure. But any reader who has made it this far will recognize that all its necessary elements have been eroded alarmingly over the past several decades. This has surely contributed to political drift, immobilism in the face of tough, divisive problems like energy and inflation, shrill single-issue politics disdaining compromise, enfeebled leadership, and growing public cynicism and distrust of politicians and political institutions.[12] Responsiveness is insufficient without responsibility. The politics of congressional elections, and the structural characteristics of Congress which they have done much to shape, produce the former but not the latter, and we are all the worse for it.

Future Prospects

This book has examined a number of trends which, if continued, portend no diminution of the problems discussed in this and the previous chapter. There are, however, a few recent signs that these trends have been halted, perhaps even reversed. A party realignment and revival may even be in the works. At the very least, some new developments are worth a few final speculative thoughts.

In 1980, the Republicans conducted a national campaign for Congress as well as for president. The campaign had a common theme ("Vote Republican. For a change.") which was obviously easy to include in any individual campaign. It had a common target, the Democratic majorities in Congress, symbolized by the figure of Speaker Tip O'Neill, who was caricatured in TV ads as an old-fashioned, free-spending backroom

---

[11] Fiorina, "Decline of Collective Responsibility," pp. 26–27.
[12] Ibid., pp. 39–44; see also the introduction to this book.

politician. There was even some suggestion of a common program, a general commitment to the Republican platform with its "supply-side" economic centerpiece, which promised the pleasure of a large tax cut without the pain of reduced revenues and thus programs. The campaign aimed at saddling Democrats in general with responsibility for the mess the country was in and offered an alternative program, however vague, to clean it up. It was an altogether sensible strategy for a party out of power at a time of economic and foreign policy failures. And there was more to it.

National-level Republican committees had raised an unprecedented amount of money to spend on congressional campaigns. The money was used not only to finance a national media campaign attacking Democrats generally, but also to support individual Republican candidates. They were not merely given the money, but also training in how to organize and conduct campaigns and professional assistance in carrying them out. The national party even intervened selectively in some primary contests in an attempt to assure that the strongest candidate was nominated. The strategy implicitly recognized that the only effective way to influence present-day congressional elections is to focus on individual candidates and campaigns.[13]

Nineteen-eighty turned out to be the best Republican year in a generation. Republicans took the White House, the Senate, and thirty-three additional House seats, enough to produce a majority for conservative economic policies when combined with conservative Democrats and to put the party within striking distance of majority control. Electoral victories were followed by legislative victories as the administration got its way on major budget and tax cuts and was able to enact its basic economic program. One key to these victories was virtually unanimous Republican support for administration programs in both houses. Meanwhile, polls were showing a rise in the number of Republican party identifiers. Party government appears to have revived with some vigor.

[13] Gary C. Jacobson, "Congressional Campaign Finance and the Revival of the Republican Party," in *Proceedings of the Thomas P. O'Neill Symposium on the U.S. Congress,* ed. Dennis Hale (Chestnut Hill, Massachusetts: Boston College, forthcoming).

Perhaps. It remains to be seen whether these are lasting phenomena or merely temporary shifts in a highly volatile political world. But there are reasons to be skeptical that anything has changed fundamentally, and there is no reason to think that underlying political divisions have healed or become coherent. First, Republican victories in House and Senate elections were very much a function of individual candidates and campaigns. The evidence for this was presented in Chapter 6. Reagan's coattails were not especially long; newly elected Republican members of Congress must be aware of how much their success was due to their own efforts.

Second, the dramatic administration victories on budget and tax legislation were not achieved easily. They required extraordinary, single-minded efforts that were assisted enormously by Reagan's personal popularity. They also occurred in policy areas where Republicans were most united as a party and where Democrats had, for the time being, run out of ideas. When it became clear in the fall of 1981 that economic problems were persisting (unemployment at 8 percent, the economy in recession, interest rates falling only slowly from record highs, the prospect of record deficits), the president's proposals for further spending cuts immediately ran into serious difficulties. Opposition came from Republicans who were beginning to worry about the 1982 elections, now only a year away, as well as from Democrats. As the budget deficit threatened to grow much larger than predicted, suggestions were made to roll back tax cuts or to impose new taxes to reduce it. The president's program commanded unanimous Republican support and not a little from Democrats as long as it seemed it might work. But it did not take long for the coalition to erode once the hope for quick success faded and members began noticing bleak economic projections for the next year.

All the work to get the economic programs in place left little time or energy to deal with other pressing problems. The AWACs sale was almost defeated, the president only saved from deep embarrassment at the last minute. Administration defense policies won less than universal support, with some of the strongest criticism from right-wing Republicans. Attempts to reduce economic regulation and to open up public lands to more resource exploration and exploitation quickly ran into formidable opposition in Congress that crossed party lines.[14] Even more divisive social issues, notably abortion, were wisely kept off the agenda as long as possible. The happy unity on the first round of budget and tax legislation was not evident on other issues.

It might be expected that Republican unity would be greater than usual because of the national party's work to elect Republican candidates. If members were not simply grateful for the help they had received, they might still be open to persuasion because of the need for future assistance. But this view ignores the reality of congressional election politics. The party's help may be welcome, but congressional incumbents certainly do not have to rely on it. They enjoy many other abundant sources of campaign funds and are in a position to raise as much as they need without help from the party. It is a lesson labor supporters of Democrats learned to their chagrin. When many Democrats elected in the early 1970s with heavy labor backing decided, with an eye to district voters, not to support legislation dear to organized labor, they could do so in full knowledge that business and trade PACs could more than make up for the loss if labor money were withdrawn.[15]

The real source of Republican unity on economic issues is ideological. If district sentiments coincide with ideological inclinations, as in the first round of budget and tax cutting, unity is easily achieved. Problems come when they clash; will Republicans vote with district sentiments or stick to principles? One way, party unity breaks down; the other way, the member risks replacement by a Democrat. Democrats have themselves chosen, on the whole, to trim their sails to the current ideological winds when state or district conditions recommend it. Are Republicans likely to do otherwise?

The willingness of Democrats to adapt to current political forces also mitigates against a sharpening of party lines and the development of party responsibility. Democrats did not op-

---

[14] California's entire Republican delegation to the House protested when Interior Secretary James Watt proposed to open scenic coastal areas to oil exploration.

[15] Crotty and Jacobson, *Parties in Decline,* p. 223.

pose a tax reduction or, indeed, many budget cuts; they simply offered alternative programs to do the same thing. Few were willing to defend Great Society programs with any vigor (after all, more than 80 percent of them had not even been around when these programs were enacted [16]). A substantial number of them went along, in the end, with the administration's economic proposals. The administration, on its side, needed Democratic votes in the House. It got some of them by promising not to support the Republican challenger actively in 1982. The short-term policy coalition was reinforced at the expense of the party coalition in the long run.

The 1982 Elections and Beyond

It is obviously too early to say whether recent developments foreshadow a major transformation in the system of electoral and congressional politics depicted in this book. No single election or Congress can define a trend; it takes several before enduring mutations can be distinguished from ephemeral variations. The 1982 elections will supply some important clues. Attention will be focused on whether or not the Republicans win control of the House. But *how* they win or lose seats will reveal at least as much about possible changes in the politics of congressional elections.

In no election since 1934 has the president's party picked up House seats at the midterm. It happened in 1934 as part of the last great party realignment. If it were to happen in 1982, it would be taken to mean that some change of comparable magnitude is under way. That might be a misinterpretation. Thomas Mann and Norman Ornstein have pointed out how Republicans could pick up seats in 1982 despite the absence of any genuine realignment. In postwar years, the president's party in the *first* term of an administration has lost an average of only twelve House seats (the average loss in the second term has been forty-six seats). Republicans should benefit from reapportionment alone with a gain of from five to ten seats. It would not take

[16] Norman J. Ornstein, "The House and the Senate in a New Congress," in *The New Congress*, eds. Thomas E. Mann and Norman J. Ornstein (Washington, D.C.: American Enterprise Institute, 1971), p. 374.

much for them to increase their representation in the House without a great alteration of traditional patterns.[17]

Mann and Ornstein also point out that Republicans will have better organization and much more money to spend than the Democrats. But if these turn out to be the telling advantages, customary interpretations of midterm congressional elections will have to be set aside. The conventional wisdom about midterm elections is that what happens depends largely on the economy and the ability of the president to retain public support. If the Reagan administration's programs brought prosperity by the fall and if no foreign policy disasters tarnished its record, for example, Republican congressional candidates would be expected to do well. At the extreme, it is conceivable that 1982 would usher in an era of Republican supremacy, with a majority of voters cheering supply-side economics the way they once cheered the New Deal.

Such a scenario lit up the dreams of more than a few Republicans in the spring of 1981. By the fall, sobering reality in the form of bad economic news and signs of some disarray in the administration's domestic and foreign policy apparatuses could not be ignored. Republicans were looking at a recession that showed few signs of ending quickly, and even administration economists were predicting 9 percent unemployment during the first part of 1982. The uncertainty (described by some commentators as near panic) among Republican members of Congress about what to do in the face of mounting economic problems reflected worries about the election a year hence. Republicans have ample reason to worry about midterm recessions; they have been there before (see the data in Table 6.1, especially 1958 and 1974).

Under such circumstances, 1982 would normally be expected to be a good year for Democrats, a bad one for Republicans. Even if voters do not necessarily vote their pocketbooks, politicians think that they do. Recall from Chapter 6 that, at present, decisions made by candidates and campaign activists, based on expectations about the forthcoming election, actually produce the conditions (in the form of differences in the aggregate qual-

[17] Thomas Mann and Norman Ornstein, "The 1982 Election: What Will It Mean?" *Public Opinion* 3 (June/July, 1981):48–50.

ity of candidates and vigor of their campaigns) that help to fulfill those expectations. Electoral prophecies are self-reinforcing. If Republicans, reading the political tea leaves, anticipated a rough year and acted accordingly, they would be likely to suffer at the polls. Democrats who expected conditions to help them recoup their losses of 1980 would pursue strategies that should, indeed, help them to attain this end.

But the money and organizational resources the Republicans assembled for 1982 (and will similarly have available for future elections) have added a new dimension to congressional election politics that could alter traditional patterns sharply. National Republican committees, enjoying the fruits of their effective fundraising operations, budgeted $26 million for Senate campaigns and $37 million for House campaigns in 1982. They also worked harder than ever to recruit strong candidates. The "identification of good, qualified Republican candidates is our main priority," reported the Republican Congressional Committee's campaign director, Joe Gaylord, early in 1982. "We have spent almost all of 1981 carrying out that priority." [18] His committee also worked to make sure that they would run, keeping up their hopes and enthusiasm despite the unpleasant economic news.

If Republicans do well in 1982 despite a recessionary economy because they are so well financed and organized that they can recruit strong candidates and give them ample campaign resources regardless of national conditions, the politics of congressional elections could change significantly. A new set of expectations might emerge, altering the strategic behavior of candidates and other congressional activists. No longer would their strategic decisions hinge on assessments of national economic and political conditions. So no longer would the choices between candidates and campaigns offered to voters at the state and district levels reflect national political forces, and no longer would voters, by responding to the choice offered, react, however indirectly, to national forces. How then could the congressional electorate act like a "rational god of vengeance and reward?"

[18] "GOP Earmarks $63 Million for '82," *San Diego Union*, January 17, 1982, p. A–18.

Bibliography

Abramowitz, Alan I. "A Comparison of Voting for U.S. Senator and Representative." *American Political Science Review* 74 (1980):633–640.

———. "Choices and Echoes in the 1978 U.S. Senate Elections: A Research Note." *American Journal of Political Science* 25 (1981):112–118.

———. "Name Familiarity, Reputation, and the Incumbency Effect in a Congressional Election." *Western Political Quarterly* 28 (1975):668–684.

Achen, Christopher H. "Measuring Representation." *American Journal of Political Science* 22 (1978):475–510.

Arcelus, Francisco, and Meltzer, Allan H. "The Effects of Aggregate Economic Variables on Congressional Elections." *American Political Science Review* 69 (1975):232–239.

Arseneau, Robert B., and Wolfinger, Raymond E. "Voting Behavior in Congressional Elections." Paper delivered at the Annual Meeting of the American Political Science Association, New Orleans, September 4–8, 1973.

Arterton, F. Christopher; Jacobson, Gary C.; Kayden, Xandra; and Orren, Gary. *An Analysis of the Impact of the Federal Election Campaign Act, 1972–1978.* A Report by the Campaign Finance Study Group to the Committee on House Administration of the U.S. House of Representatives. Institute of Politics, John F. Kennedy School of Government, May, 1979.

Barone, Michael, and Ujifusa, Grant. *The Almanac of American Politics 1982.* Washington, D.C.: Barone and Co., 1982.

Bibby, John F.; Mann, Thomas E.; and Ornstein, Norman J. *Vital Statistics on Congress, 1980.* Washington, D.C.: American Enterprise Institute, 1980.

Bloom, Howard S., and Price, H. Douglas. "Voter Response to Short-Run Economic Conditions: The Asymmetric Effect of Prosperity and Recession." *American Political Science Review* 69 (1975):1240–1254.

Born, Richard. "Changes in the Competitiveness of House Primary Elections, 1956–1976." *American Politics Quarterly* 8 (1980):495–506.

————. "House Incumbents and Inter-Election Vote Change." *Journal of Politics* 39 (1977):1008–1034.

Bullock, Charles S., III. "Redistricting and Congressional Stability." *Journal of Politics* 37 (1975):569–575.

Burnham, Walter Dean. "Insulation and Responsiveness in Congressional Elections." *Political Science Quarterly* 90 (1975):411–435.

Campbell, Angus; Converse, Philip E.; Miller, Warren E.; and Stokes, Donald E. *Elections and the Political Order.* New York: John Wiley, 1966.

Cavanaugh, Thomas E. "The Two Arenas of Congress: Electoral and Institutional Incentives for Performance." Paper delivered at the Annual Meeting of the American Political Science Association, New York, August 31–September 3, 1978.

Clapp, Charles L. *The Congressman: His Work as He Sees It.* Washington, D.C.: Brookings Institution, 1963.

Clem, Alan L., ed. *The Making of Congressmen: Seven Campaigns of 1974.* North Scituate, Massachusetts: Duxbury Press, 1976.

Cnudde, Charles F., and McCrone, Donald J. "The Linkage between Constituency Attitudes and Congressional Voting Behavior: A Causal Model." *American Political Science Review* 60 (1966):66–72.

Congressional Quarterly. *Electing Congress.* Washington, D.C., 1978.

Conway, M. Margaret, and Wyckoff, Mikel L. "Voter Choice in the 1974 Congressional Elections." *American Politics Quarterly* 8 (1980):3–14.

Cover, Albert D. "One Good Term Deserves Another: The Advantage of Incumbency in Congressional Elections." *American Journal of Political Science* 21 (1977):523–542.

Cowart, Andrew T. "Electoral Choice in the American States." *American Political Science Review* 67 (1973):835–853.

Crotty, William J., and Jacobson, Gary C. *American Parties in Decline.* Boston: Little, Brown, 1980.

Cummings, Milton C., Jr. *Congressmen and the Electorate.* New York: The Free Press, 1966.

Davidson, Roger H., and Oleszek, Walter J. "Adaption and Consolidation: Structural Innovation in the House of Representatives." *Legislative Studies Quarterly* 1 (1976): 37–66.

———. *Congress and Its Members.* Washington, D.C.: Congressional Quarterly Press, 1981.

Davidson, Roger H., and Parker, Glenn R. "Positive Support for Political Institutions: The Case of Congress." *Western Political Quarterly* 25 (1972):600–612.

Deckard, Barbara Sinclair. "Electoral Marginality and Party Loyalty in House Roll Call Voting." *American Journal of Political Science* 20 (1976):469–481.

———. "Political Upheaval and Congressional Voting: The Effects of the 1960s on Voting Patterns in the House of Representatives." *Journal of Politics* 38 (1976):326–345.

Decision Making Information and Hart Research Associates. *A Study of the Impact of the Federal Election Campaign Act on the 1976 Elections.* Prepared for the Federal Election Commission, Washington, D.C., 1977.

Dodd, Lawrence C., and Oppenheimer, Bruce I. *Congress Reconsidered.* 2d ed. Washington, D.C.: Congressional Quarterly Press, 1981.

Edwards, George C., III. *Presidential Influence in Congress.* San Francisco: W. H. Freeman, 1980.

———. "Presidential Influence in the House: Presidential Prestige as a Source of Presidential Power." *American Political Science Review* 70 (1976):101–113.

Ehrenhalt, Alan, ed. *Politics in America: Members of Congress in Washington and at Home*. Washington, D.C.: Congressional Quarterly Press, 1981.

Erikson, Robert S. "The Advantage of Incumbency in Congressional Elections." *Polity* 3 (1971):395–405.

———. "Constituency Opinion and Congressional Behavior: A Reexamination of the Miller-Stokes Representation Data." *American Journal of Political Science* 22 (1978):511–535.

———. "The Electoral Impact of Congressional Roll Call Voting." *American Political Science Review* 65 (1971):1018–1032.

———. "Is There Such a Thing as a Safe Seat?" *Polity* 9 (1976):623–632.

———. "Malapportionment, Gerrymandering, and Party Fortunes in Congressional Elections." *American Political Science Review* 66 (1972):1234–1245.

———. "Measuring Constituency Opinion: The 1978 U.S. Congressional Election Survey." *Legislative Studies Quarterly* 6 (1981):235–246.

Erikson, Robert S., and Wright, Gerald F., Jr. "Policy Representation of Constituency Interests." *Political Behavior* 1 (1980):91–106.

Eulau, Heinz, and Karps, Paul D. "The Puzzle of Representation: Specifying Components of Responsiveness." *Legislative Studies Quarterly* 2 (1977):233–254.

Fenno, Richard F., Jr. *Congressmen in Committees*. Boston: Little, Brown, 1973.

———. *Home Style: House Members in Their Districts*. Boston: Little, Brown, 1978.

———. *The United States Senate: A Bicameral Perspective*. Washington, D.C.: American Enterprise Institute, forthcoming.

Ferejohn, John A. "On the Decline of Competition in Congressional Elections." *American Political Science Review* 71 (1977):166–176.

Fiorina, Morris P. "The Case of the Vanishing Marginals: The Bureaucracy Did It." *American Political Science Review* 71 (1977):177–181.

———. *Congress: Keystone of the Washington Establishment*. New Haven: Yale University Press, 1977.

————. "Economic Retrospective Voting in American National Elections: A Micro Analysis." *American Journal of Political Science* 22 (1978):426–443.

————. *Representatives, Roll Calls, and Constituencies.* Lexington, Massachusetts: D. C. Heath, 1974.

————. *Retrospective Voting in American National Elections.* New Haven: Yale University Press, 1981.

————. "Short- and Long-Term Effects of Economic Conditions on Individual Voting Decisions." *In Contemporary Political Economy,* edited by D. A. Hibbs and H. Fassbender. Amsterdam: North Holland, 1981.

————. "Some Problems in Studying the Effects of Resource Allocation in Congressional Elections." *American Journal of Political Science* 25 (1981):543–567.

Fishel, Jeff. *Party and Opposition: Congressional Challengers in American Politics.* New York: David McKay, 1973.

Fowler, Linda L. "Candidates' Perceptions of Electoral Coalitions." *American Politics Quarterly* 8 (1980):483–494.

Frantzich, Stephen. "Opting Out: Retirement from the House of Representatives, 1966–1974." *American Politics Quarterly* 6 (1978):251–273.

Froman, Lewis A., Jr. *Congressmen and Their Constituencies.* Chicago: Rand McNally, 1963.

Goldenberg, Edie, and Traugott, Michael. "Congressional Campaign Effects on Candidate Recognition and Evaluation." *Political Behavior* 1 (1980):61–90.

————. "Normal Vote Analysis of U.S. Congressional Elections." *Legislative Studies Quarterly* 6 (1981):247–258.

Goodman, Saul, and Kramer, Gerald H. "Comment on Arcelus and Meltzer, The Effect of Aggregate Economic Conditions on Congressional Elections." *American Political Science Review* 69 (1975):255–265.

Hale, Dennis, ed. *Proceedings of the Thomas P. O'Neill Jr. Symposium on the U.S. Congress.* Chestnut Hill, Massachusetts: Boston College, 1982.

Hershey, Marjorie Randon. "Incumbency and the Minimum Winning Coalition." *American Journal of Political Science* 17 (1973):631–637.

————. *The Making of Campaign Strategy.* Lexington, Massachusetts: Lexington Books, 1974.

Hibbing, John R., and Alford, John R. "The Electoral Impact of Economic Conditions: Who Is Held Responsible?" *American Journal of Political Science* 25 (1981):423–439.

Hinckley, Barbara. "The American Voter in Congressional Elections." *American Political Science Review* 74 (1980):641–650.

———. *Congressional Elections.* Washington, D.C.: Congressional Quarterly Press, 1981.

———. "House Re-Elections and Senate Defeats: The Role of the Challenger." *British Journal of Political Science* 10 (1980):441–460.

———. "Incumbency and the Presidential Vote in Senate Elections: Defining Parameters of Subpresidential Voting." *American Political Science Review* 64 (1970):836–842.

———. "Interpreting House Midterm Elections: Toward a Measurement of the In-Party's 'Expected' Loss of Seats." *American Political Science Review* 61 (1967):694–700.

———. "Issues, Information Costs, and Congressional Elections." *American Politics Quarterly* 4 (1976):131–152.

Hinckley, Barbara; Hofstetter, Richard; and Kessel, John. "Information and the Vote: A Comparative Election Study." *American Politics Quarterly* 2 (1974):131–158.

Huckshorn, Robert J., and Spencer, Robert C. *The Politics of Defeat.* Amherst, Massachusetts: University of Massachusetts Press, 1971.

Hurley, Patricia A., and Hill, Kim Quaile. "The Prospects for Issue Voting in Contemporary Congressional Elections: An Assessment of Citizen Awareness and Representation." *American Politics Quarterly* 8 (1980):425–449.

Hutcheson, Richard G., III. "The Inertial Effect of Incumbency and Two-Party Politics: Elections to the House of Representatives from the South, 1952–1974." *American Political Science Review* 69 (1975):1399–1401.

Jacobson, Gary C. "The Effects of Campaign Spending in Congressional Elections." *American Political Science Review* 72 (1978):469–491.

———. "The Impact of Broadcast Campaigning on Electoral Outcomes." *Journal of Politics* 37 (1975):769–793.

———. "Incumbents' Advantages in the 1978 Congressional

Elections." *Legislative Studies Quarterly* 6 (1981):183–200.

———. *Money in Congressional Elections.* New Haven: Yale University Press, 1980.

———. "Practical Consequence of Campaign Finance Reform: An Incumbent Protection Act?" *Public Policy* 24 (1976): 1–32.

———. "Presidential Coattails in 1972." *Public Opinion Quarterly* 40 (1976):194–200.

———. "Public Funds for Congressional Campaigns: Who Would Benefit?" In *Political Finance,* edited by Herbert E. Alexander. Sage Electoral Studies Yearbook, Vol. 5. Beverly Hills, California: Sage Publications, 1979.

———. "Strategic Politicians and Congressional Elections, 1946–1980." Paper delivered at the Annual Meeting of the American Political Science Association, New York, September 3–6, 1981.

Jacobson, Gary C., and Kernell, Samuel. *Strategy and Choice in Congressional Elections.* New Haven: Yale University Press, 1981.

Johannes, John R., and McAdams, John C. "The Congressional Incumbency Effect: Is It Casework, Policy Compatability, or Something Else?" *American Journal of Political Science* 25 (1981):512–542.

Jones, Charles O. *Every Second Year.* Washington, D.C.: Brookings Institution, 1967.

———. "Inter-Party Competition for Congressional Seats." *Western Political Quarterly* 17 (1964):461–476.

———. "A Suggested Scheme for Classifying Congressional Campaigns." *Public Opinion Quarterly* 26 (1962):126–132.

———. *The United States Congress: People, Place, and Policy.* Homewood, Illinois: Dorsey Press, 1982.

Kayden, Xandra. *Campaign Organization.* Lexington, Massachusetts: D. C. Heath, 1978.

Kernell, Samuel. "Presidential Popularity and Negative Voting: An Alternative Explanation of the Midterm Congressional Decline of the President's Party." *American Political Science Review* 71 (1977):44–66.

Kiewiet, D. Roderick. "Policy-Oriented Voting in Response to Economic Issues." *American Political Science Review* 75 (1981):448–459.

Kinder, Donald R., and Kiewiet, D. Roderick. "Economic Discontent and Political Behavior: The Role of Personal Grievances and Collective Economic Judgments in Congressional Voting." *American Journal of Political Science* 23 (1979):495–527.

Kingdon, John W. *Candidates for Office: Beliefs and Strategies.* New York: Random House, 1968.

Kostroski, Warren Lee. "Party and Incumbency in Postwar Senate Elections: Trends, Patterns, and Models." *American Political Science Review* 67 (1973):1213–1234.

Kramer, Gerald H. "Short-Term Fluctuations in U.S. Voting Behavior, 1896–1964." *American Political Science Review* 65 (1971):131–143.

Kritzer, Herbert M., and Eubank, Robert B. "Presidential Coattails Revisited: Partisanship and Incumbency Effects." *American Journal of Political Science* 23 (1979):615–626.

Kuklinski, James H., and McCrone, Donald J. "Policy Salience and the Causal Structure of Representation." *American Politics Quarterly* 8 (1980):139–164.

Kuklinski, James H., and West, Darrell M. "Economic Expectations and Mass Voting in United States House and Senate Elections." *American Political Science Review* 75 (1981):436–447.

Leuthold, David A. *Electioneering in a Democracy: Campaigns for Congress.* New York: John Wiley, 1968.

McLeod, Jack M.; Brown, Jane D.; and Becker, Lee B. "Watergate and the 1974 Congressional Elections." *Public Opinion Quarterly* 41 (1977):181–195.

McPhee, William, and Glaser, William A., eds. *Public Opinion and Congressional Elections.* New York: The Free Press, 1962.

Maisel, Louis Sandy. "Congressional Elections in 1978: The Road to Nomination, the Road to Election." *American Politics Quarterly* 8 (1981):23–48.

———. *From Obscurity to Oblivion: Congressional Primary Elections in 1978.* Knoxville, Tennessee: University of Tennessee Press, forthcoming.

Maisel, Louis Sandy, and Cooper, Joseph, eds. *Congressional Elections.* Beverly Hills, California: Sage Publications, 1981.

Malbin, Michael J., ed. *Parties, Interest Groups, and Campaign Finance Laws.* Washington, D.C.: American Enterprise Institute, 1980.

Mann, Thomas E. *Unsafe at Any Margin: Interpreting Congressional Elections.* Washington, D.C.: American Enterprise Institute, 1977.

Mann, Thomas E., and Ornstein, Norman J., eds. *The New Congress.* Washington, D.C.: American Enterprise Institute, 1981.

Mann, Thomas E., and Wolfinger, Raymond E. "Candidates and Parties in Congressional Elections." *American Political Science Review* 74 (1980):617–632.

Mayhew, David R. *Congress: The Electoral Connection.* New Haven: Yale University Press, 1974.

―――. "Congressional Elections: The Case of the Vanishing Marginals." *Polity* 6 (1974):295–317.

Miller, Arthur H., and Glass, Richard. "Economic Dissatisfaction and Electoral Choice." Manuscript. Center for Political Studies, University of Michigan, 1977.

Miller, Clem. *Member of the House.* New York: Scribner's, 1962.

Miller, Warren E., and Stokes, Donald E. "Constituency Influence in Congress." *American Political Science Review* 57 (1963):45–57.

Nelson, Candice. "The Effects of Incumbency on Voting in Congressional Elections." *Political Science Quarterly* 93 (1978/1979):665–678.

Ornstein, Norman J., ed. *Congress in Change: Evolution and Reform.* New York: Praeger, 1975.

Paletz, David. "The Neglected Context of Congressional Campaigns." *Polity* 3 (1971):195–218.

Parker, Glenn R. "The Advantage of Incumbency in House Elections." *American Politics Quarterly* 8 (1980):449–464.

―――. "Interpreting Candidate Awareness in U.S. Congressional Elections." *Legislative Studies Quarterly* 6 (1981): 219–234.

―――. "Some Themes in Congressional Unpopularity." *American Journal of Political Science* 21 (1977): 93–109.

Parker, Glenn R., and Davidson, Roger H. "Why Do Americans Love Their Congressmen So Much More than Their Congress?" *Legislative Studies Quarterly* 4 (1979):53–61.

Payne, James L. "The Personal Electoral Advantage of House Incumbents, 1936–1976." *American Politics Quarterly* 8 (1980):465–482.

Peters, John G., and Welch, Susan. "The Effects of Charges of Corruption on Voting Behavior in Congressional Elections." *American Political Science Review* 74 (1980): 697–708.

Piereson, James E. "Presidential Popularity and Midterm Voting at Different Electoral Levels." *American Journal of Political Science* 19 (1975):683–693.

Ragsdale, Lyn. "The Fiction of Congressional Elections as Presidential Events." *American Politics Quarterly* 8 (1980): 375–398.

———. "Incumbent Popularity, Challenger Invisibility, and Congressional Voters." *Legislative Studies Quarterly* 6 (1981):201–218.

Rivers, Douglas, and Rose, Nancy L. "Passing the President's Program: Public Opinion and Presidential Influence in Congress." Paper delivered at the Annual Meeting of the Midwest Political Science Association, Cincinnati, Ohio, April 16–18, 1981.

Schantz, Harvey L. "Contest and Uncontested Primaries for the U.S. House." *Legislative Studies Quarterly* 5 (1980):545–562.

Schoenberger, Robert A. "Campaign Strategy and Party Loyalty: The Electoral Relevance of Candidate Decision Making in the 1964 Congressional Elections." *American Political Science Review* 63 (1969):515–520.

Stone, Walter J. "The Dynamics of Constituency: Electoral Control in the House." *American Politics Quarterly* 8 (1980):399–424.

———. "Measuring Constituency-Representative Linkages: Problems and Prospects." *Legislative Studies Quarterly* 4 (1979):623–639.

Snowiss, Leo M. "Congressional Recruitment and Representation." *American Political Science Review* 60 (1966):627–639.

Sullivan, John L., and Uslaner, Eric M. "Congressional Behavior and Electoral Marginality." *American Journal of Political Science* 22 (1978):536–553.

Tufte, Edward R. "Determinants of the Outcomes of Midterm

Congressional Elections." *American Political Science Review* 69 (1975):812–826.

——. *Political Control of the Economy*. Princeton, New Jersey: Princeton University Press, 1978.

——. "The Relationship Between Seats and Votes in Two-Party Systems." *American Political Science Review* 67 (1973):540–554.

Tidmarch, Charles M. "The Second Time Around: Freshman Democratic House Members' 1976 Reelection Experiences." Paper delivered at the Annual Meeting of the American Political Science Association, Washington, D.C., September 1–4, 1977.

Uslaner, Eric. "Ain't Misbehavin': The Logic of Defensive Issue Strategies in Congressional Elections." *American Politics Quarterly* 9 (1981):3–22.

Weatherford, M. Stephen. "Economic Conditions and Electoral Outcomes: Class Differences in the Political Response to Recession." *American Journal of Political Science* 22 (1978):917–938.

Westlye, Mark C. "Information and Partisanship in Senate Elections." Paper delivered at the Annual Meeting of the American Political Science Association, New York, September 3–6, 1981.

Wolfinger, Raymond E., and Rosenstone, Steven J. *Who Votes?* New Haven: Yale University Press, 1980.

Wolfinger, Raymond E.; Rosenstone, Steven J.; and McIntosh, Richard A. "Presidential and Congressional Voters Compared." *American Politics Quarterly* 9 (1981):245–255.

Wright, Gerald C., Jr. "Candidates' Policy Positions and Voting in U.S. Congressional Elections." *Legislative Studies Quarterly* 3 (1978):445–464.

——. "Constituency Response to Congressional Behavior: The Impact of the House Judiciary Committee Impeachment Votes." *Western Political Quarterly* 30 (1977):401–410.

——. *Electoral Choice in America*. Chapel Hill, North Carolina: Institute for Research in Social Science, 1974.

Yiannakis, Diana Evans. "The Grateful Electorate: Casework and Congressional Elections." *American Journal of Political Science* 25 (1981):568–580.

Index

211